Best Wishes from
Wayne Curtis

Of Earthly and River Things

Also by WAYNE CURTIS

Fiction

Night Train to Havana

Monkeys in a Looking Glass

River Stories

The Last Stand

Preferred Lies

One Indian Summer

Non-Fiction

Long Ago and Far Away

Wild Apples

River Guides of the Miramichi

Fishing the Miramichi

Currents in the Stream

Poetry

Green Lightning

WAYNE CURTIS

Of Earthly and River Things

AN ANGLER'S MEMOIR

Edited by Rebecca Leaman.
Cover image after a work by Michael Gil, flickr.com.
Cover and page design by Julie Scriver.
Printed in Canada.
10 9 8 7 6 5 4 3 2 1

Library and Archives Canada Cataloguing in Publication

Curtis, Wayne, 1943-
Of earthly and river things: an angler's memoir / Wayne Curtis.

Also issued in electronic format.
ISBN 978-0-86492-661-6

1. Curtis, Wayne, 1943-.
2. Authors, Canadian (English) – 20th century – Biography.
3. Miramichi River Valley (N.B.) – Biography.
4. Fishers – New Brunswick – Miramichi River Valley – Biography.
I. Title.

PS8555.U844Z47 2012 C813'.54 C2012-902799-5

Goose Lane Editions acknowledges the generous support of the Canada Council for the Arts, the Government of Canada through the Canada Book Fund (CBF), and the Government of New Brunswick through the Department of Culture, Tourism, and Healthy Living.

Goose Lane Editions
500 Beaverbrook Court, Suite 330
Fredericton, New Brunswick
CANADA E3B 5X4
www.gooselane.com

For my grandsons, Joshua and Samuel

Contents

A Dam in a Grove

I remember clearly one evening in late April, when my father took me to the dam to fish. I had only a twig for a fishing pole, some coarse black thread for a line, and a twisted safety pin for a hook. We had gone to the garden after a shower and dug up a few angleworms, and I distinctly recollect Daddy pulling them from the stubborn earth, putting them into a bottle of soil, and punching holes in its cover to keep them from suffocating. We walked across the rain-moistened field, where our retired horse, Muggins, cropped turf that still had snow along the tree-shaded line fence, to a spot where the Cavanaugh Brook trickled through a grove of tall poplars.

While, at the time that I went there with my father, the fishing hole was known as "the dam," what remained of that structure was in fact nothing more than a few mossed-over logs that lay across the brook with water trickling under them.

This was just a stone's throw from where my great-great-aunt Sarah's plank home had stood a century before; its crumbling rock foundation still remained. That old tree-shaded farmhouse was where she lived her entire life, working as a dairymaid, and where she died of rheumatic pains in November 1888. This was the brook from which she carried her household water in iron-banded wooden buckets, and in the spring of the year, according to my father, a few wild trout for the breakfast frying pan. As we walked, Daddy pointed to Aunt Sarah's sunken footpath, still visible under a network of dead grass and brambles.

In the grove Daddy baited my hook. And when I dropped it into the water under an overhanging sod, I got a nibble, straight off! I held my breath, and the sounds of my heart beating filled the silent woods. It was as if, for the moment, the line and even the twig had come to life. A good solid jerk, a vigorous pull, and a pan-size speckled trout was dancing in the dead leaves, the hook already having dropped from its mouth.

I scrambled to get hold of the fish. And I can remember its desperate movements as it wiggled and slipped forward in my hands, its expanded blood-red gills resembling the underside of a mushroom. I could see down its throat, past the gaping mouth with heart-shaped rows of teeth like needle points. Daddy said that it was more than likely a fish he had caught in the main river years before and had carried in a bucket of water to release into the pond behind the dam.

My first instinct was to put the trout back into the brook, quickly, before it died, or put it in a pail of water and carry it to the river for a safe release. But Daddy said that the trout's growth had already been stunted, its skin darkened from having lived in the backwater so long, and that, because it had grown old here, it would not likely survive in the more competitive main stream. On the other hand, if we fished awhile longer, we might catch a few more to take home and fry up and serve with molasses and homemade bread for breakfast as our aunt Sarah used to do, and which has long since become a spring tradition in our family. Still, I wondered how big my fish would have grown had it been left to feed in the big waters where it belonged.

We visited a few more little pools without a nibble, and then I broke an alder crutch to use as a carrying stick, after stringing my trout on it by the gills. My mother had seen us coming across the yard and was standing in the kitchen door, my baby sister in her arms. A savoury smell of freshly baked bread drifted from the room behind her.

"Oh my good-ness look at thisss!" she came forward to give me a hug. (My mother always spoke slow and deliberate, breaking the words into syllables when she was trying to make something seem important.) Pictures were taken: my father and I standing together with the trout, and me alone, crouching beside an old sawhorse, the fish laid out on the dead grass in front of me. It was the only trout that I can remember bringing home while fishing with Daddy, the only such shared celebration.

In bed that evening, in those long moments before sleep—a time when I would otherwise have been nervous, even asthmatic in that dark room alone—until mother came and tucked me in and gave me a good night kiss, my thoughts were still in the grove. And I felt guilty for not thanking the Powers Above for my good fortune in catching that big trout. I scrambled out of bed, knelt down on the board floor, and prayed to Jesus, St. Mary, St. Paul, St. Peter, and all the other Bible people I had crayoned in the Sunday school colouring book, until my conscience was clear.

After this prayer was finished and I had said my now-I-lay-me-down-to-sleep and drifted off, I dreamed that I was riding Muggins—a horse that wore the golden shoes of a retired king—across our fields toward the dam. When the old horse stumbled and almost fell, I sat up and grabbed the rungs of the bedstead. "Whooa!" I shouted. Once I realized I was back in my bedroom and safe from danger, my mind filled with memories of the trout incident, the dam, and the grove. I could not get back to sleep. I tossed and turned while grasping and holding once more that squirming trout with its red and pink and yellow speckles, and its orange belly that was cold and slippery as the sole of a wet moccasin. An air of triumph filled the darkened room. I cannot recall when, in reality, I went back to the dam, though I suppose I did so the next evening.

Later that fall, when I was in grade one, I went to Newcastle with my father and he bought me a number-one steel trap: a single-spring, square-jawed device with a silver chain and ring, the word Victor engraved on its pan. Daddy said that it was "good for catching mink and weasel." That evening, with a can of sardines for bait, we went again to the grove, where my father punched holes in the tin so that the juices leaked out; then he nailed it to a tree near the brook. He built a little house of sticks around the bait and placed the trap in the entrance with some dead leaves covering it.

He told me to keep an eye on the trap but not to go too close, as my scent would warn off any wild animal. Every day after school I went there, stood at a distance, and looked at the set. But as far as I can remember, no animal, big or small, ever came to the trap, which after a few weeks of fall rain, started to corrode to the point that the scent of rust must have overpowered the bait. So the trap, which by then had become frozen into the ice, was taken up with the prying of a crowbar, the idea abandoned. I didn't want to kill an animal anyway, just as I had not wanted to kill the trout. It was a pet I was looking for.

But from that time forward, the dam, and indeed the grove where the dam existed, became a place to escape the displeasures invoked by farm chores and allergies and to be solitary with nature, in real life and in dreams. And this, I believe, was not because it represented a big part of my father's ideology, the dreams he'd had for the dam and the grove years before—he had developed it in part as a place to woo my mother with a different view on life than the one that she and I would later share. No, Daddy's vision was one of working the land, of taking what the streams, woods, and fields had to offer him whereas my interest (like Mum's) in the stream and the grove was for their beauty, the tranquil state of mind they offered to anyone who was sensitive enough to notice that they were to be enjoyed and not destroyed. Certainly not by flooding a section of the grove, as father had done to create a fishing pond for mother, a woman who believed that all streams should flow without destruction. Yes, we had loved the grove for opposite reasons; although I doubt if I really understood this until many years later.

In school I would daydream about being in that grove. In my mind, it offered a series of little pleasures that I felt would be incommunicable to my father. Even now, I believe a person is transformed into adulthood, whatever its shortfalls, by the places and events of one's earliest memories. For I clearly remember the grove's converging paths, the ferns and bracken, the giant, tar-banded trees, some of which had fallen from decay to become long, moss-covered sponges that were difficult for me to climb over. The birds, insects, and small animals abounded around the chuckling brook, which to me was—and still is—a symbol of freedom.

Downstream from the grove, in the old fields, there were high banks on each side of the brook, where in early spring the runoff combed the dirty blond grass into waves. These stood against the sunlight like thatched roofs. Sometimes, for excitement in the spring, my older brother Winston set fire to these hillocks, creating a brown-grey smoke that drifted across the tilled fields, impregnating the air with sweet incense and turning the setting sun into a red beach ball. The blaze left map-shaped patches of ash, which after the rains, turned green, and then blue with the quick-sprouting violets. The fragile stems of these flowers were moist and transparent, their downcast velvety bells wilting under my awkward touch, leaving blue dragonfly-wing patterns on my hands. Winston always burned in the evening hours, after the winds had died and there was little chance the fire would spread into cultivated grounds. Sometimes the burning began after darkness set in. Spring grass fires were common back then, and I can still see the scattered and zigzagging blazes, leaping here and smouldering there, as they made their way forlornly over the unruly marshlands where last summer's mowing machine could not have reached, and which could have been hacked free of wild rushes only by the long blade of my grandfather's scythe. I can still feel those sweet-smelling spring winds, the draft that the blaze created, taste the ashes that bring back my shortness of breath, the sweat and tears of inland toil, the smoking fields of spring, the burnt-out end of that bygone day.

But in the grove there was no burning, and on the ground lay a cushion of dead leaves. The brook was crystal clear and no more than thirty centimetres wide. In places it was hidden completely as it trickled beneath overhanging sods of green and grey moss, and its clay bottom was smooth, like putty under a pane of glass. The water in the Cavanaugh Brook was always ice-cold as it was fed from a big spring, well back on the maple-treed hillside of my uncle's farm.

As we grew, my sister, my brothers, and I, along with our cousins from the next farm, spent more and more time in that brook. Barefoot and freckled from the spring sun, we waded about its swampy ponds. As the days passed we observed, as the cattail shoots broke through like green thumbs from beneath the dead leaves, and the floating frog spawn jelled, ever so slowly. We trapped the pollywogs, the baby toads, and snakes in the palms of our muddy hands. And then we set them free.

In the lower swamp, where the brook was all but stopped because grandfather had not been able to get there with his digger to open the channel and let it run freely—an annual summer chore—there were ponds the colour of steeped tea, and the trees' roots were exposed upon the forest floor like veins on the feet of a storybook giant. While the season advanced toward autumn, there was the strong scent of bog as we balanced ourselves on these roots and stretched to keep our ankles dry as we grasped for the tall, twisted, multi-layered stems of cattails that emerged from the water, the brown, cigar-shaped blooms on top our eternal quest. Each cattail had a spear on its blossom end, like the flagpole on top of the Empire State Building. Hurrying home before dark on Halloween, we dipped these wick-like sponges into our parents' oil drum and used them for torches, before unravelling their burning down to scatter and create a make-believe roadblock of sparks on the gravel highway that led to the village.

When the brook flooded from the November rains and ponds lay in the fields dappled with frozen cow manure, when the temperatures dropped so sharply that the swamp became a patchwork of white ice that resembled preserver's wax, and the little, more shallow pockets sparkled in reds and greens between the roots, the whole concern looked like a leaded, stained glass window. We took snow shovels to cut off the cattail stems and used them, along with alder skeletons, to feed our evening bonfires. Sparks scattered into the moonlit heavens, and the ice on which we skated turned into a plate of amber porcelain, making kinked dancing shadows of the over-clothes mummies we had become to keep warm.

But the poplar grove was where my father had established his fishing pond years before. The dam was made of overlapping, split-cedar poles driven into the ground at an underwater slant, the way beaver dams are built, so that the more water that gathered in the compound, the tighter the structure became. Then, to improve the landscape, Daddy pruned and thinned out the trees around the pond, which stretched out for quite a ways beyond our line fence. For romantic reasons, because he had a big date coming up, he even moored an old canoe there for a while.

This was where my father took my mother to fish in the spring before they were married. (They wed on Christmas Eve 1938.) It was an outing Daddy had promised his lover months before; one that she understood, because of the excitement in his voice, was going to be in a much more exotic place. She had travelled a bit more than him, had worked as a chambermaid in Fredericton and in Newcastle, and was a step above him socially. Still, according to Mum, when she got there, disappointed though she was, she good-naturedly put on my father's long rubber boots and followed him along that little stream. She swatted flies and stopped here and there to drop a baited hook into the water, while grasping his hand to be led this way or that through a tangle of underbrush. As they poked along, bumblebees buzzed among the new-leafed trees and the scarlet-breasted robins ran on the ground, their songs audible—bee answering bee, bird answering bird—against the trickle of the dam's overflow.

"It was like the whole thing had been contrived by your father to make an impression, send me a message," my mother told me years later.

"And those little violets down there by the brook were the same blue as your mother's eyes," Daddy put in, and he pulled down the corners of his mouth, as he always did when he was teasing her. Of course, my mother's eyes were brown.

When they stopped to rest, Daddy stood on a stump and told jokes, which he laughed at himself, claiming they were spontaneous, but she found out later he had memorized them from a gramophone record. Then in his shrill, flat voice he sang a few of his comical old cowboy ditties. This, Mum learned in time, he would always do in places where he had an audience of one or more.

"I was so embarrassed I blushed to the roots of my hair," she recalled. "I just could not look at the man!" My mother was a woman who had no time for the frivolous.

Later in the day, Daddy helped his date into the canoe and together they paddled about the backwater, stopping occasionally to gaze upon the new life the spring and the pond were bringing forth and which gave her the warm and passionate feelings that she had expected from the visit. These were subtle impressions, like the fragrances of expensive perfumes, lost perhaps on the senses of my father, a countryman who took such trivial things with a grain of sand.

In the shadows of evening, they fished in the trout-stocked

pond, until the water reflected a big rising moon, and the singing of toads and the peeping of baby frogs became more audible as darkness approached.

Daddy told me many times that the pond, the canoe, and even the stocked fish "had been to impress your mother, a million-dollar woman! But anything more would have happened as a result of letting nature have its way, in the spring."

For them, this experience grew more romantic with the passing years, the cloak of time, and of course the embellishment that came with the telling and retelling.

Years later, while helping my father in the hayfields, I stole away to that grove where the dam had been, to lie on my belly and slurp up the ice-cold water that made my teeth ache. And to escape the dust-laden breeze of the season, the brown smoke of puffballs broken by the tines of the pitchfork, the shortness of breath that I suffered from the miseries of hay fever. I reclined in the shade of those old dark trees while the sun slanted through foliage that rustled without a breeze. My major faults were, according to Father, indolence and my love of nature. He admonished me for whiling away my hours and not living up to his expectations. Of course, he did not understand my world of allergies, my solace in nature and in books. I was my mother's son in that she was a constant reader of novels, her favourite author being Daphne du Maurier, with whose name she had christened my sister. Sometimes my mother went to that solitary place to meditate and to read, on afternoons when she had a need to get away from her dull household routine.

And if I saw her there—sitting on a log with a book in hand—I would stay away until after she had left the spot.

There among those trees I could smell the pungent poplar bark and the sour stench of mud after a shower, hear the murmur of the wind up high among the leaves. I could watch the drifting clouds that stirred my imagination—the ragged and oversized sheep that the wind transformed into fat polar bears and then into circus tents. And on the horizon, tremendous heaps of vanilla ice cream and cotton candy. I related these images to those in "The Cuckoo" or "Into My Own" or some other school poem by William Wordsworth or Robert Frost.

These images and the feelings they inspired have carried the memories of that old place and time right through the years, so even now they are symbols of a youthful state of mind and impregnable solitude, which I associate with the grove where the dam was. Old-school poetry and prose—a place in the mind. Shady woods and a cooling stream—a place in the heart. And I can hear and feel them both, high in the elm trees of my city street or whispering among the graveyard flowers on my walks in the old church grounds.

Even now, so many years later, at the first light of dawn, I sometimes awake to a nostalgic moment, when I am back at my childhood home. There is the rattling of stove covers in the kitchen below my bedroom, a signal from my father that there are morning chores: cattle to feed, eggs to collect, and stovewood to carry into the house for my mother's cooking day—jobs that are no longer there for me, except in the mind, where all past experiences are embedded forever.

I get dressed in my best winter clothes and walk a city block to The Grill for a cup of tea and a doughnut. I sit at the counter and enjoy the home-cooked flavours, which conjure memories of the old pasture just as it appeared when I drew back the curtain of our kitchen window to witness the slow, cold rain of November, and beyond, the silence of the woods where I so often helped my father cut firewood, which Muggins hauled to the shed for me to stack in tiers. And the poplar grove returns, too, always a haven from the workload, the allergies. Again I can feel the presence of my father as he rests an arm on my shoulder and walks with me across the old home fields toward the dam. I see my mother blush as he sings in his little, shrill voice, "Let Me Call You Sweetheart" or "Down by the Old Mill Stream." And for a moment we are all back together, not in body, certainly, but in whatever it is that endures within us. Yes, it is all there in the taste of a doughnut. And I think I want to go back, build a cottage upon Aunt Sarah's cellar wall, right over the wild raspberry vines that carry so many tangled ancestral memories.

But now, too, in addition to these musings—and I suppose because of the aging process—my recollections of that old place and time have become harder and harder for me to grasp and hold. Like a dream that remains untold. They are scattered like pieces of old brick and dinner plates I suppose I could still find among the bramble of Aunt Sarah's cellar. Some of the events are murky and I cannot put a finger on the date. Others are mythical and I cannot say for sure if they happened to me or if I only heard about them long ago. I do know that my strongest attachment to the dam and the grove were in those years when I was between five and eleven, before I was allowed to go to the river.

In his middle age, my father, with whom I had so often been disagreeable, told me he felt a responsibility to teach me how to use the same implements that his father had shown him when he was a boy: the fish hook, the steel trap, the pitchfork, the axe, the milking stool, because some things should not change, especially if they were from the previous generation. According to him, the new ways were less important than tradition, a belief that—like the lessons of church and school—held all good families together.

Later on, it seemed as though he better understood my predicament. He admitted that he was glad I had developed an interest in such subjects as biology and especially botany and that I had no interest in killing anything bigger than a mosquito. As for the books, he said that he understood my love for them because my mother had been a reader. But these declarations came only in his last days, when he had become mellow. Before that he had no time for such impracticalities. He was his father's son in that regard.

I understood how he had followed his father's teachings and that his father had followed his father and so on. For it was the way of countrymen with their sons and of countrywomen with their daughters. It was the expected legacy that ran through all families. And I understood, too, why my father was disappointed that I had followed more closely to my mother's way of thinking. She was always saying she wanted me to make something of myself, that I had to reach higher to avoid complacency, and no internal rewards came with mediocrity. Mum believed that darkness was the symbol of ignorance and light represented knowledge. Eventually, I discovered that her light was really my light and that we both suffered from each other's darkness. And I promised myself I would do the very best that I could in school and around home to see that her wishes were fulfilled, not to spite him for sure, but for my own quality of life. Those secret codes between my mother and me were unbroken to the end.

Still, Daddy was one of the most affectionate men I ever knew; throughout his long life, he harboured a wealth of kindness and goodwill toward all people. He was a romantic at heart, a singer and a painter of landscapes, but he had been trained by his father to be more practical in the rural sense—to tackle the manual side of the workload, first and last. He was also a bit conservative in his ways. In his old felt hat (tilted over one ear) and wool sweater (neatly buttoned), his presence was like an overwhelming conscience that I can feel, even now, as I write this.

On the day of my father's funeral, I stood by his graveside and I thought of the dam he had built so long ago and how he had taken my mother there to impress her with his creativity and his showmanship. I thought of the spring evening when he took me to the dam for the first time and how the memory of that little outing stood up right through the years.

I remembered it, I supposed, because I believed that he had wanted me to follow him and his old family ways. Certainly at that age I wanted that too. And then I thanked the God of my childhood for my father's priorities. I had learned so much about the brook and its species and life itself because of that little fishing trip. It was only then, on the day of his funeral, that I realized my father had planted a seed I would nurture the rest of my life.

And I was lonesome as hell for my old man.

Open Water

Long before the ice left the river, there were patches of open water along the shore across from home. This was where the little spring-fed brooks trickled into the main stream and thawed the snow and ice, even in the wintertime. These air holes and pieces of bare shore grew larger as the sun strengthened until, on a day in early spring, there came a subtle change in the wind, or the landscape, or something unseen, which my brothers, my sister, our cousins from the next farm, and I could feel in the air. And this roused something inside us, so that without uttering a single word, we set about rummaging through old sheds and barns for last year's fishing gear and from the attic closet a few pieces of spring clothing.

We fell together at the riverbank, from where we moved like a gust of wind toward the wire bridge, made our way across on the shaky spans, and hurried on the crusted snow along the opposite side to where that narrow stretch of water lapped choppy and black against the shore. There we stood at the water's edge, tied to our fishing line a newly created streamer—hen feathers attached to a sailor's safety pin—and cast it into those deep currents in hopes of catching a spring salmon.

This experience was not so much about the place we had escaped to, a cold and drab setting at that time of the year, where a harshness of winter elements was still present; it had more to do with the carefree spirit that existed around that patch of open water, which on damp mornings expelled a cloud of fog that hung over the shore and hillside like a cocoon. This was an atmosphere composed of the fish and water smells, the river breezes that were gentle, though chill, the wind-tossed trees, and the bright early spring sunshine that each of us had been dreaming about through the long, cold winter, and which triggered fantasies of much more exotic escapism. As if the place were some kind of bottomless wishing well, the kind we read about in our school readers, where a giant talking goldfish appeared each day to grant us our deepest and most heartfelt wishes.

Such musings were common among us river children. Our young, overactive imaginations could spin to fantastic proportions, ignited by the most ordinary moments and the sense of freedom that would have been incommunicable to the more worldly kids, who grew up in urban places. Indeed, our view of the outside world at that age was restricted to the confines of old-school geography, which offered very few pleasurable destinations.

After school and on weekends, my brothers, sister, cousins, and I went to the river each day. In the spring of '52, when I was nine years old and we were quarantined from school because of the fear of smallpox, we lived at the river. With our handmade juniper rod, fish twine, and homemade fly hook, we hurried to get to that open water, which was clean and bright before the spring rains began. So narrow was the stretch that, even casting from the shore as we were, it was possible to reach the standing ice.

Of course it was illegal to angle in the main river before the ice went out; in those days, "ice-out" was the time when the season officially opened. Still, anxious to get started after the dreary winter and fuelled by "spring fever," we made our way to the mouth of McKenzie Brook. We built bonfires on the broadening patches of bare ground, sat on a bench at the water's edge, smoked tobacco or the shore's dead grass, and being overly polite with one another—because we wanted everyone to have a good time—took turns casting. Just being there meant that our angling season had started long before anyone else in the country even dreamed of catching a salmon.

Our casts became longer as the air hole widened, the standing ice melting gradually into a honeycomb of crystals, as the penetrating sunshine made pink and red reflections of the crusty prisms, so vivid yet so short-lived, while the sun shone through ragged clouds in shafts of gold. Then it dropped into the tree-topped horizon in the bend of the big frozen river.

It was as if, more than anything, we just wanted to be near the water, to drink it from our palms, wash our hands, chapped from the cold wind, and turn our faces toward the strengthening sun, absorb the river breezes almost a month before the ice cover had left the water. Actually, the days were warmer before the ice went out. There was less dampness, the wind less biting than it would have been if the whole river had been open, especially there in the lee of those big old trees. Away from the woods at the water's edge after ice-out it was always three or four degrees colder.

I can still see my little sister, Daphne, huddling with the boys, her unruly hair an autumn-leaf yellow where it projected in sprigs from under her home-knit, stocking-leg cap, and my cousin Marion, who was afraid of eels, and whose eyes beneath the furry hood of her winter parka were as blue as an evening sky before a thunderstorm.

The fact that it was not even spring but we were at the river, with its marine smells, and smoking the tobacco-tasting dead grass, made us feel like we were reliving the most poignant of moments in the most significant of places. And in the way of country children, forever doubtful about being accepted, we valued our friendships and the little social cliques that grew, wanting one another to stay at the river and not to give up on that inner travelogue—because it had been a group package. We shared the fishing rod with a measure of generosity and a new-found concern for one another.

"Here, lemme show ya how it's done!"

"Just two more casts."

"Okay. Okay. Then I'll show ya how."

"Gimme a tailor-made cigarette will ya? No, I wanna 'nother cigar, a big cigar!"

We fished with good-natured banter and cranked in many salmon. Big fish, too. We never tired of this, for each fish hooked was a new experience, a unique moment in our childhood. (They could have been broadbill or marlin or tuna, and we might have been fishing off the coast of Havana or Key West or Cayo Largo.) But this was not all about fishing, or indeed the joy of having found this patch of open water, so much as it was about sharing that internal escape, the dream world each of us lived inside ourselves. And each spring brought with it internal growth of the older ones who reached back for nostalgic excitement no longer there, while the younger ones reached forward to adventures not yet experienced, changing our developing personalities, which have since carried us through life, each in different directions, from the places we loved most. For there is an old river wisdom that states, "We are linked, not so much by who we are, but where we dream to be."

We stood with one rubber boot in the water and cast our hen-feathered streamer well out toward the crusted and blue-shaded ice that was still thick enough to hold up a horse at that time of the spring. And we dipped our rod into the current to free the guides from the build-up of ice the breezes had created. We observed the winds that we knew would blow the hook in or out of the fish's mouth, depending upon which way it was coming, down or up that open stretch. The bad-luck crosswinds would blow a fly hook toward our eyes or ears in the back-cast, especially if we were fishing on a Sunday, because our parents told us that it was a sin to fish on the Sabbath unless we were hungry and needed a fish for the table. This was particularly true if we hadn't gone to church that morning. We tried to keep our feet dry as we let the fly swing, long and deep, all the while anticipating the big pull from below.

When the pull came, and the hook was set, we knew we had

a black marlin, a broadbill, or a tuna on the line—depending on who was holding the rod. There was a lot of scampering about and shouting to the fisher to keep the tip up, to stay strong in the harness, brace your feet against the bridge, sway the line this way or that, while leading the fish away from the standing ice, until the salmon started to splash about, revealing its back and then its sides and finally its belly, tinted yellow from the dark water, and we were able to steer it up on that shore of mud and dead grass.

Late March to early April was a good time to fish for the spring salmon, as they were hungry after their long winter under the ice. Those big fish lay along that bend in eddies three metres deep. And I can still feel the fishing line as it tightened and vibrated. I can still see its long slant into water that reflected aqua, and then purple, and then lavender through the lenses of the childish sunglasses we had bought at Underhill's Five-and-Dime Store in Blackville. Our crooked and kinked images mirrored us, standing upon our heads in the water. As we cranked in our fish, we talked to one another in foreign accents, "Wait til my friends in New Yaaak see this onnnee." And we took photos with the make-believe cameras we all carried in our imaginary fishing vests.

A dark cloud made shadows that moved with the wind along the ice and the water, while hailstones hissed and hopped on the exposed and brittle shore grass like ice worms in a dance. Behind us, the leafless elm trees offered a roost for the noisy first crows and blackbirds that appeared as if from out of the branches. And somewhere back on the forested hillside the chestnut-sided warbler sang, "Please, please, please ta meet ya."

One evening a giant otter, as black as coal, ran out from among those trees. It splashed into our fishing hole, did two somersaults on the surface, let out a screeching snarl, and crawled to sit upon the standing ice. Then, as if to show us how it was done, it dove to the bottom, muddied the water, and came up with an eel between its jaws before disappearing under the ice cover, never to be seen again.

"Wow, did you see that?"

"Yes... no, I didn't see nothing."

"Then it must have been a forerunner."

"I saw it. It was a kangaroo."

"What?"

"A kangaroo."

"DAPHNE SAW A KANGAROO!"

We fished until well after dusk had drifted over the river like a brown fog, and we felt the raw loneliness—in ourselves and in one another—that came with the dampness, the hollow chill of murmuring water, and the darkness of the woods, as though we were sharing a premonition from an as yet unheard of tragedy, the fatal illnesses that so often followed those twilight fevers brought on by the measly east winds, which carried the disease that kept us from school. We stamped out our cheerful campfire and half-carried, half-dragged our catches as we headed up the shore toward home, slumping along on the rotting crust, experiencing the same letdown that a child feels when Christmas morning is suddenly over.

We tramped into the kitchen and stood by the stove to warm away the river chill, the bonfire and shore grass-tobacco smell that had become steeped into our clothing. To please our mother and father, we adjusted our speech back to our own from the put-on accents of the American sports because they had expressed some concern about this new lingo we had picked up at the shore. And our mother scolded us for sometimes stealing our father's tobacco.

"Oh-h, go-o-dd He-av-ens, what will become of yuz? And look at yer hands!" She rubbed our wind-chapped palms with camphorated oil. Then she said, "Now come to yer suppers."

Mum had fried a few of those black salmon steaks in butter, after battering them in flour. We ate them with homegrown potatoes, the peelings left on, and her homemade green-tomato chow chow and country biscuits sweetened with molasses, gourmet dishes fit for some of the finest lodges on this or any other river in the world.

Later, after the lamps were blown out and the house was silent and cool because only a low fire burned in the kitchen stove, we wandered off to our bedrooms. After we said our prayers, those big fish swam in our dreams, each of us in our own little world. And the two settings—the glorified inner cinema that unravelled from the hype of just being able to throw a line so early in the season and the drab harsh world of the river itself still under a layer of thick ice—became scrambled in a hodgepodge of fantasy. We tried to measure one against the other, the imaginative against the natural, with the realization that we needed the abstract and the real, both of which we had lived that day.

The morning came with a cold, spectacular sunrise that touched our faces through the curtainless windows—my mother was doing her spring cleaning and the curtains had been taken down—and we jumped from our beds and dressed while scrambling down the stairs to the kitchen. (The first one out of bed was the best dressed, having put on the least worn clothes that belonged to a sibling, still asleep.) We hurriedly ate our porridge and baked beans, picked up our rod, and made our way down along the shore on the shiny, frost-hardened crust, which overnight had turned yesterday's heel marks into porcelain saucers, and across the bridge to that grove of trees and the patch of open water that grew broader and longer as each day passed.

We fished with this dedication until, one afternoon near mid-April, we noticed little wakes toward centre stream, ever so subtle, coming from the standing ice. It was then we heard a great thumping and churning on the river. And we could see that our patch of open water was getting smaller and smaller. Fast. We reeled in our lines and hurried to the riverbank where we watched as the big white slab that covered the river broke into smaller triangles and rectangles with rifle-shot-like precision, and as bushed trails, water-filled horse tracks, and pale blue skating rinks with their half-burnt car tires and rusted wires—all imprints from the winter's activities—pushed against our sodden shore. And there were hollow freshet sounds, the pouring of water against ice. A breeze tossed the pine boughs, as if the wind and the water worked as one. The river frothed and churned until the ice jam had covered our fishing hole, footpath, plank seat, the campfire and grass-cigarette ashes, before it came to an abrupt stop. We ran down the shore, climbed the steps, and hurried across the bridge, just in case the ice jam caught in the cables and swept them away, for we knew this sometimes happened during the spring freshet.

On the bridge, which was oh so close to the ice by then, we could see the jam had left a strip of open water on our side. And on this water there were a few wild ducks already swimming about.

"Look," my sister said. "The river is all open on this side! Our fishin' trip is not over, we can fish along here."

"No, no, no. It's too dangerous!" I told her. "That crust is shaded and slippery. Do ya wanna slide into the water and drift right down under the ice and never be seen again?"

The shore's red dogwood shrubs, purple-blossomed alder, and the white-along-black-stem pussy willow had suddenly become surrounded by the fast-moving water, which was brown like urine in a chamber pot. So, empty-handed and feeling dejected because we had lost our fishing hole and indeed our dream world, we hurried home to tell our parents what had happened.

"Don't let me catch yuz anywhere near it!" Mother snapped.

"Once the ice swings over in the bend that way, it don't stay long. She'll be gone in a day or two," Daddy assured us.

He was right of course. The next morning when I awoke, I could see the big open river as I had seen it the year before from my schoolhouse windows (when the teacher scolded me for not paying attention to what was happening in class). An upriver wind made the water sparkle so dark a blue with the little white crests riding the tops of the waves and with miniature icebergs adrift in the currents. Because the river had risen in the night with the ice run and then had dropped again, there was a ridge of white crust along each shore like the outer matting that frames a piece of riverscape artwork. An eagle, like a giant kite, circled above the trees of the far hillside.

As if they had—like the crows and blackbirds—come out of the elm-treed interval overnight, there were motorboats. Their whining engines and the bark of voices filtered through our ill-fitting window panes. The guides were hunched down behind their straw-haired, out-of-country guests, who were better dressed and better spoken than any of us, but who were looking to feel a fish on the end of a line just as we had done a month before. Dressed in many layers, they were propped up in the boats like the stuffed men we set on verandas for Halloween, their faces a candy-apple red from the sun and the water and the wind.

That wind always came with ice-out. It was a sharp, cold breeze that ruffled the feathers of nesting ravens, stiffened laundry on clotheslines, carried the scent of grass fires, and rippled the stagnant field ponds. It stabbed through our new spring jackets, while jerking the kite strings from our hands. These gales made it difficult for the guides to anchor and hold their canoes so the foreign sportsmen and sportswomen (perhaps reliving their own winter illusions), could let out the expensive lines and cast, troll, mend, and retrieve their custom-made streamers, while they drank hot tea spiked with rum from Thermoses and smoked Cuban cigars with a new-found simplicity of heart, like they were just glad to be here. This, no doubt, had been their once-a-year vacation. And they laughed too loud and too often. Through the day we could hear them from where we sat in our drafty backhouses. We learned to laugh like them: it was a ghostly chuckle, carried on the wind, like that of a distant loon.

In a sense, our river had become their river, though perhaps for opposite reasons. For them angling our spring salmon—which to us children had become old-shoe by then—was an escape into the wilderness to find themselves, just as we had stretched our imaginations to reach into their world. Had they wanted to be one of us? Had they envied us our river? Had they begrudged us our river savvy and freedom, at least for the moment? I think so. For us, the river experience had nourished our dreams, visions of a better life far away. For them, it was a big-city dream they had come to our open waters to make real.

And yet, we had been trying to live inside the sport fishers' world all this time. The salmon we had on the line, which in the practical sense meant no more to us than a sack of potatoes or a bushel of beans, was more valued for what it brought to us in the way of a fantasy, the big pull from below. Still, the fish that we were cranking in were worth a million dollars to the community because of the excitement they brought and the escape factor they created, not only in our minds, but also in those of the foreign sport fishers who spent so much money to come here all the way from "New Yaaak." It was good to know the river had returned for everyone, even the sport fishers. Especially the sport fishers because our fathers and mothers worked as outfitters, river guides, and camp cooks. Everyone wanted to see them have a good time and come back next year with their pockets full of money.

Once they arrived, each day at suppertime we ran to the river to stand on the wire bridge and look down into the snub-nosed motorboats that passed so closely beneath us, driven by our fathers and uncles. The sport fishers pointed to us and laughed and called us "natives."

Sometimes they stopped the boats and we came to the water's edge where they took our pictures, asking us to pose in a row like a ragged grade three class. We jostled with one another to keep from standing in the front, like when we were going to the school nurse for a needle to prevent smallpox. For the moment, I was glad that we were not common school children just then, that we had been quarantined and not in a classroom doing all the proper things. Wasn't this life more interesting? Wasn't it more original? Wasn't it more creative and inspiring than a mediocre school day? Would there be a better way to dampen our fun, put a harness on our lively imaginations than to be disciplined in a classroom?

"Here ya go kids, get yourselves a Popsicle!" They pass us some change.

"I don't want a Popsicle. I want a fly hook, that red one in your hat."

"Here ya go kids, a fly hook foor yuzzz." The American turns to his guide, "They say red is the colour for us to use!"

"Then red is the colour," Uncle Eldon tells him.

We had gone to the river just to see if they'd caught any fish.

Spring Waters Run Deep

As a schoolboy, I had been taught to honour my mother and father, just like the Bible said, "So that your days may be long in the land." I also celebrated a more remote ancestry whose portraits were in gilded frames in our living room. Life's experiences—some of which came to me second-hand, in stories—taught me to revere and glorify our river, fields, and woods, as well as the sun, wind, and rain, because our livelihood depended upon all these things. I learned to respect the horses, cows, and chickens that lived in our barnyard, along with the fish, animals, and wild birds that inhabited the forest and streams surrounding our home—all were sacred to us country children. We were a part of everything, and everything, including the landscape, riverscape, and sky, was a part of us. Indeed, respect for our river community and its inhabitants was the creed we all lived by, or tried to live by.

There were sparkling streams, salmon and trout for pursuing, fields of grain and potatoes for harvesting, giant trees for sawing into logs for the mill, rainstorms of biblical proportions, days out of doors where we heard a church bell on the wind, and the sun burned my bare shoulders at haying time. These things were shared by family members, some of whom were long dead, their old coats hanging in attic closets, their voices audible when darkness came.

My home community of Keenan is on the Miramichi, a river system that flows from the heart of New Brunswick northeast to the sea. Said to be the best salmon river in the world, she is beautifully dressed, spirited yet modest, sometimes to me even sentimental in her sounds and scents. (For I am a heart person, an Aquarian, and my love for the river elicits these feelings.) This is where my ancestors settled when they emigrated from England in 1818; they went to school here, lumbered, farmed, and fished. And now they sleep in country churchyards. I have followed in their footsteps, in an abbreviated and nostalgic way, documenting wherever possible their rugged but romantic past. The river has always played a big part in the livelihood of my family; it still does. But now, much of the influence is spiritual. The moods and sentiment the river inspires still nourish the manifestations of old home and kinship.

In those last days of winter, when I was a lad, every evening after school I went to the river to see if the patches of open water had grown a bit bigger since the day before. I stole along on the decaying crust that crumbled like road salt and spilled into my boots as I followed the interminable tree-lined paths that were speckled with spruce needles which became more difficult to travel on each day because of their disintegration—only to find that the river ice had decayed but a fraction from the day's warming winds. Even at that age—I was ten years old—going there was a form of meditation for me, an escape to a river that, despite its ice cover, was full of wonderment. And I tried to relate my own river experiences to the school-book waters of Mark Twain, E. Pauline Johnson, and Joseph Conrad. For sure, there seemed to be a sense of freedom and adventure in all of them. I still look at rivers that way.

By the early spring the river was crusted over and looked like the face of the moon, its ash-like craters honeycombed from the sun into flakey prisms. As I watched and waited for the ice to move out, I looked forward to the new riverscape; for the river was always changing, physically and metaphorically—from the spirited, freshet sounds of high spring, to its lazy summer cadence, to the bony trickling waters of autumn, the silence of winter—each stimulating my curiosities, a fresh starting point for a new season of adventures.

I waited patiently through bad weather as the open water expanded, inch by stubborn inch, its potential as a play area signified by the noises of the earth: the crows hollering, the winds whispering in pine boughs, the freshet sounds of cider-coloured brooks that rushed downhill to flood our shores. The ice-scarred alders and skeletal lupine stood like a row of pen strokes at the high-water mark, where a hush of evening sunshine cast monstrous shadows upon the decay, with night falling fast and cold among the trees and in the lee of farm buildings.

As springtime advanced oh so slowly, I watched for the river to break out of its shell, and I hoped that it would not happen during the night. As a river child, I knew the ice would go with a giant crash and a great outpouring of force; this was a spectacle

I did not want to miss. At that stage in my life, the river was like a piece of artwork I could not treasure fully because I was standing too close to it. Or perhaps I lacked the sophistication. And yet, I appreciated it well enough to understand that under its cover of ice it had a mind of its own, and everything would move in its own time, its own intended direction. I knew I would be vitalized by its spirit just as water in a vase nurtures a wildflower.

I watched until the rains came and melted away the last snow of winter. The big ice jams crowded our shores and scraped the bark from our bank trees. Fields and the low, wooded flats flooded. The adults talked of so-and-so's shed, a wire bridge, and a damn good boat going adrift in the night.

Finally, the open river flowed in a state of peacefulness, fringed with straw-coloured grass that slanted downriver among heaps of flint that stood along our shores like poorly chiselled polar bears. Then came the gas-smelling motorboats that spilled their pastel curls on the water under plumes of drifting smoke. Their passing, so close, wrinkled the water and threw muddy waves upon the rubber boots of those of us who stood with a line in the eddy, hoping for a spring chub or a trout.

Early on, I had ordered an eight-foot steel rod, a reel with a two-handle crank, and a level casting line from the Eaton's of Canada mail-order catalogue. I had tied up a few streamer fly hooks from deer hair and the hen feathers I gathered in my father's barn. Having sent to the game warden's office for a fishing permit, I awaited its arrival in the mail. Such was the pastime of a lad growing up too far from town to be involved in organized sports. Still, I was thankful that I was living in a place where the property's greatest value was measured by its proximity to the river, not in dollars, but for me, in adventure.

And I often wondered how the older village teens, so near yet so far removed from that scene, could exist without the presence of the river in their lives. Would the love of baseball and tennis keep me from the shore? Was my river considered countrified? Was there a class distinction? To me, it appeared as though they felt the river was a symbol of hard times—a place to work the log drive, to get a day's guiding, a fish for the table—even though it was no less wonderful where it ran past their homes, for all our villages were on the river. They chose to spend their evenings at a smoky diner where a jukebox and a soda fountain were the attractions, and the conversation was about motorbikes and cars and girls. Among the young women, there was talk of boys, boys, and more boys. I was not in that place because of my age, and in the spring of the year the unpaved roads were impassable. To go to the village, I'd have had to walk eight kilometres through deep woods on an abandoned railway line.

In school, visions of the river played in my mind and made the long, boring hours a bit more endurable. Indeed, the river had become a place where longing took me to escape arithmetic, solving problems, and memorizing old-world poetry. After the ice left the river, it was hard to stay in school, harder still to concentrate on long division or the War of 1812.

In my days out of school, I kept an ear to the river while helping my father to dismantle the bobsleds before the truck-wagon was backed out of the barn to sit in the rain-sodden dooryard, or while we assembled the harrows and the seeders for the spring planting. Yes, always a workload, but the call to freedom, too, that beckoned just beyond the hill; even from my bedroom windows at night, especially at night, when all river sounds became hollow and amplified by the darkness, I could hear it.

Sometimes, after school and on weekends, my friends and I gathered at the river and we fished from the cable bridge, built bonfires in pits of rock on the shore, smoked tobacco, and huddled in the lee of old boats from the upriver wind. We jostled and joked in profane limericks while we cast as far as we could, to get those homemade streamers swinging into the heavy currents. We cast and watched for the doughnut-shaped splash that the black salmon made, and a split second later, when the fish hit, we felt the pull from the depths of those moving waters, so far out that our fishing lines strained like bowstrings. We cranked with vigour as we ran downstream and leaned into our bending rods to pick up line, until the fish had tired and we could, ever so carefully, reach into the icy water to retrieve it. Those old kype-jawed spring salmon were giants to drag onto the grass, hold in our slimy hands, then set free to swim away and be caught another day.

Of course, we sometimes ate those fish, especially during Lent and on Good Fridays. But our real motivation was to observe and enjoy the coming of spring, to play the season while it lasted. And to gain what excitement we could out of that April river, bonded together there, against the elements, challenging the water, the wind, and the fish.

Later in the spring I went to the river alone. I cast across waters that swirled over amber gravel, where the ghosts of fish swam, vague and shadowy as in a dream. Reflections of the sun's rays danced as the upriver breeze caught the water's surface to make moving patches of ink. When I saw a splash at my hook, felt a tug from below, I responded with a pull and cranked in a pan-size speckled trout, its yellow belly flashing under the surface. I cast again, and again, but without another rise. The sun moved off the river and lit up the opposite shoreline, then the hillside, and then the distant treetops before disappearing into the horizon at dusk. And I moved to the deeper, slower, and more promising waters.

After sundown, the pollen-covered Cavanaugh Eddy became dark and mysterious, its waters filled with a sense of mystery, so that when I got a tug on my line, I could never be sure what it was. I bait-fished there and through the month of May caught fish of all sizes, from late spring salmon, to big chub and trout, to gaspareau, shad, and eels, the latter of which held stubbornly to the bottom and had to be pulled onto the shore with strong arms and added vigour.

By that time in May, the shore was sandy and warm, the small shoreline birches, having stood naked through the spring rains, were breaking into leaf. All was shaded by an aged pine tree as big around as a puncheon and so tall that it made my head swim to look up at its top branches, where an eagle sometimes roosted. Against the steep-banked side hill, the old tree's exposed roots—all splintered from the ice floes—made a labyrinth of elbows, knees, and reaching arms that curled inward to where a woodchuck had its den. A grassy sod hung over the tangle of roots like unruly hair over the pop-eyed face of an elderly fisherman.

Under that tree there was a spirit of good times that went back at least three generations. It was as if this spot offered a sweetening of my true feelings toward the old home and family. It was in the tree, it was in the sand, it was in the voices of birds; it was everywhere. The Cavanaugh Eddy was where my father and mother fished while on their honeymoon in 1938—Mum in her khaki blouse and below-the-knee skirt and Daddy in his riding breeches and Humphrey Bogart-style felt hat. In later years my family gathered there for our annual May "eat-out" on Victoria Day. We built a bonfire in the rocks and cooked. If it was raining, to keep the tradition alive we fashioned a lean-to out of tarpaper and poles and lunched under the roof. The ground was blackened by the ashes of age-old picnic parties. The family had kept the holiday for canoeing, picnicking, and trout fishing, until my parents passed away soon after the turn of the twenty-first century.

As I fished there, the spirit of my ancestry lingered in the shadows of that massive tree and watched my every move, as if to ensure my success and my eventual safe return. The aromas of those picnic parties—ham and fried eggs, homemade country breads, and hot bush tea—struggled against the scents of bird cherry and hawthorn blossom. These fragrances were replaced in June by the sweet commencement winds rustling the lilac trees.

There at the eddy, everything spoke to me of nature, of virtue, and of happiness. These were important to me, as I felt no one of them could exist without the other two. Love pulsed in my veins, for the family, and yes, for someone as yet to be found. I was still at the age—approaching puberty—when I felt a strong sense of honour toward my folks, both of whom also appreciated those wonderful spring evenings that were passing so quickly, and which I knew would never come again. Even then, I felt I was not getting all I should out of those days because there was so much to do, so few boyhood hours left in what I had been told were the best years of my life.

I stayed on the shore until long after dusk drifted in and the river turned to yellow and then to red and then to a bed of moving tar, because my father had told me it was just before dark that the big trout came in close to shore and they would take my bait. I was careful never to leave too early; I felt an obligation to take home a few fish to justify my hours away.

When I saw the line that slanted downward into the dark, smoky waters move outward in jerks, I lifted the rod with a sense of anxiety; I had used a semi-drifting bait as my father had instructed me to do. The fish held strong to the bottom and made the rod's tip bounce, so I knew it was not an eel, but a good big trout because the bottom-feeders were slow moving, less combative. Sometimes for excitement, to bring in the eels, I baited my hook with chub. The eels swallowed this bait and were dragged upon the shore like big, open-mouthed green snakes.

As I fished, the shades of night fell upon the river like a mirror and the misty-haloed moon brought its own reflections. I could hear the splash of shad and sometimes a beaver; the whole river was alive at that time of the evening.

At dusk, in the sand at the water's edge, I built a fire of grass and sticks. The orange blaze leaped into the evening sky and the sweet-scented smoke curled around me like a child's hair in a wind. I could see the fire's upside-down reflections dancing against the river's bottom, an underwater blaze reaching into the currents, until grey ashes had gathered over the dying embers. Before I left, I doused my blaze with the same water it had inflamed.

Some spooky night bird cried from the treetop, "Is that you Wayne? Is that you Wayne?" And then answered itself with a resounding note, "It's Wayne. It's Wayne. It's Wayne, Wayne, Wayne."

The brooks and the night creatures became more audible in the darkness. There was a feeling of rawness, as though my senses became more active; although I saw less at that time of day, I felt more.

"Whew! Whew!" the night bird called, as if it were a cuckoo warning me of the passing hours.

I carried my fish home and placed them in a pan of water in the warming closet, high over top of a cold stove in the outside shed. When my father came out to look at them, even though my catch was small, he said, "Holy smokes, look at all the fish! Where did you catch them?" He said this, even though of course, he knew. I remember thinking how thoughtful it was of him to feel that he had to compliment me. And for this I was proud of him. I had stayed on the river too long and half-expected a scolding.

After my father's kind words, I knew I had been forgiven for not coming home until after dark, when it was no longer possible to do my outside work; someone in the family had picked up the slack for me. My fish now served the family as a peace offering for keeping me away. So, in that regard they were much more than fish, just as the Cavanaugh Eddy had been more than a fishing hole.

I fished the eddy every evening until the pine needles, warmed by the sun, saturated the air with the smell of rosin, the tilled fields spilled forth the odour of newly turned sod, and the river winds filled with the fragrance of field flowers. It was then, when the waters warmed, that the spring salmon began to jump and leave the river to return to the sea.

And the sea-run trout came in, splashing in the fast water, along with the smelt and the gaspereau and the shad.

By then—the last week in May—the bright salmon had also begun to migrate in from the sea, with the Rocky Brook Run coming first, so consistently we could mark our calendars by them. And I changed my fishing spot to the faster and shallower waters, pursuing the new sea-run fish with smaller hooks, a more delicate cast, and a stronger concentration of strategy, even psychology. For I had learned to think like a fish by then.

I had learned all there was to know about how to contemplate the river, observe its seasonal patterns, pit my instincts against it. Much of this savvy I picked up from my mother and father. Even now, some of this knowledge serves me in good stead.

One could do worse than to grow up on a river.

At Papa's Rock

As youngsters, my friends and I spent countless hours in the river at Papa's Rock, and in the fields and woods nearby. Barefoot and suntanned, we followed the heart-shaped cow tracks along my father's pole fence—it became a water stickle at the river's edge—and slid down the leaf-littered embankment on the seats of our trousers to the gravel bar, where we huddled, smoked tobacco, drank tea in the fresh air, and watched the water for a fish to rise. Then we waded to our waists in a river that was sprinkled with May rain, the big silver drops dappling the water, one, two, three... and we cast a fly hook well out, letting it swing through the ripples of the great rock, eagerly anticipating a "strike" with each line thrown.

In the early spring, when the grass was first showing green between the bricks in our front walkway and buds were swelling on the statuesque old river elms, through the summer days of hazy cloud with their sleepy smells of new-mown hay, to the cold rainy days of autumn when high winds stripped the multi-coloured leaves from the branches, reducing those ancient trees to charcoal sketches on a nettled hillside, we were still there, standing to our hips in water, casting away, taking turns with the fly rod.

It was called Papa's Rock after Flora "Papa" Keenan, the community patriarch. This was the place where, many decades before, Mr. Keenan and his neighbours (my grandfather among them) had speared and netted salmon for "table use" in the spring and summer and fall salmon for the salt barrels and for smoking in winter.

This was where I cast a number six Oriole fly hook into the boils of the rock, hooked and landed my first bright salmon. Ever. It was the morning of June 4, 1951, and the salmon was a ten-pound Rocky Brooker. I was eight years old.

Through that late spring and early summer, and many subsequent angling seasons, I fished there with my brothers and sister, and our friends from across the river. We did not have a boat and we didn't have wading boots; but for children who used a drafty New Brunswick outhouse in the dead of winter and who bathed in the river any time after the tenth of May, the water was not totally unbearable. In fact, the anticipation of catching a salmon overshadowed any discomfort we suffered.

My friend Harold Campbell had a pair of thin rubber sock-waders that an American sportsman had given him, and because he secretly wore these under his blue jeans, he was able to outlast me in the cold water. We fished like two prospectors panning for gold, and if we got a salmon—we often did—we dragged it down the flat and across the wire bridge to the Campbell side, to a place where a cow plank bridged a small stream at the edge of the woods. There we cleaned and divided our catch, letting the spring water run through the pink inner lining of its belly before cutting the fish in half. Because our fathers and mothers had told us that a salmon was needed for supper that evening, we each hurried home with our share.

When I arrived at our farmhouse with a fish or half fish, my father would say, "God be praised, ya got one did yuz? Well, well, well! Ya did good. Now, take it inside to your mother like a good lad!" Then he would add, "I knew there was a run of salmon coming in when I saw the seagulls flying up the river."

"Seagulls?"

"Yessir."

"But ain't seagulls the sign of a big storm down the coast?"

"Yes. But they also tell us the fish are coming in. Seagulls and nighthawks!"

"Nighthawks?"

"Yessir."

"How many? I didn't see..."

"I saw them. One or two. Go in now to yer mother."

Like grandfather, Daddy always looked to the birds and animals to tell him what was happening in the way of fish runs, or what kind of weather we'd be having in the days ahead.

When I took the fish into the house, my mother said, "Oh myy heaav-enns, would ya look at thisss!"

We started fishing bright salmon as soon as the water on the bar dropped low enough so that we could wade out and reach the rock with a cast. (Long legs were an asset then.) This was around late May, early June, when we could hear the first cowbells on the flat, and the potato seeds were being put into the ground; I was freed for a day from my grade six class to help with the planting.

After a back-breaking stint in the fields, we stole away to that special place where the scent of fish and water was strong in the air. Papa's Rock. We spent the late afternoon and evening casting, casting, waiting for a rise. We stayed until it was so dark we could not see our fly hook hit the water, and lamps were lit in farmhouse windows. River sounds grew louder as darkness fell upon us and an early summer moon with its romantic intuitions rose in the sky. Toads sang on the water, and the splashes of shad and salmon were audible even from the tarpapered lean-to the old people had built on the shore a month before as a shelter for gaspereau fishing. We went there to get out of the rain and to smoke cigarettes, exchange our backhouse comic books of Roy Rogers and Dale Evans, and share in the profane stories of Pat n' Mike.

We had one good fishing rod between us, my Monique Sunbeam split bamboo, which I had cut a cord of pulpwood to buy. We took turns with it. In the cool days of autumn, after being in the water for some time, we retreated to the shelter to warm our legs by a bonfire of shore hay and driftwood, over which we brewed tea in a tin pail. One of us warmed while the other fished, and I can recall the numbness in my legs from the cold waters of September, and the emptiness, both spiritual and physical (which lasted for days), that came with the hunger and disappointment I felt after a salmon, so nearly landed, broke free. The experience of having a bright salmon on the line filled my chest with a pounding heartbeat that resembled the pulse of a live bird you hold in your hand. For us, a fish outsmarted, hooked, and landed constituted a yardstick by which we could be measured and which earned us praise from our parents. A salmon was a great treat to a family that sometimes struggled to make ends meet. But it was the acceptance I craved as much as anything, and years later, this same need for approval held me on course as I pursued bigger goals in the wider world.

When Harold and I broke a rod tip—a thing we did many times—we repaired it by whittling through the varnish on the split end and burning out the chrome-coated, steel ferrule, heating the cement and applying it evenly onto the wood, before putting it all back together with pliers. Then we'd run the still-warm ferrule through our hair or along the sides of our noses to oil it, reassemble the rod, and continue fishing. We always carried pliers, a stick of ferrule cement, matches, and a pocket knife because the tips of those old hexagon rods snapped easily, especially if it was cold and we were struggling to cast against those dark upriver winds.

When we got hungry, we climbed the hill to Harold's family's place. In their big, barn-like summer kitchen with the wall studs and rafters steeped in a century of smoke and sooty cobwebs, a pot of cooked potatoes stood on the back of the woodstove and black salmon steaks sizzled in a frying pan. We helped ourselves, flavouring the fish with molasses and swabbing our dishes clean with a piece of fresh-baked bread. We sat on a bench at the long plank table and drank black tea from chipped enamel mugs.

The Campbell's outside kitchen was filled with the ghosts

of many hard-set traditions, and the homely scent of work and sweat was ingrained into the whitewashed, fly-spattered walls where the tips of rusty nails poked through in wavering rows. It was a place where any kind of pretension would have been detected a mile away, and hungry as we were, we would never take a second helping. Not until we were invited to do so. Twice. But we did not have to be coaxed to eat the homemade blueberry pie made from the berries that had been hand-picked in the fields that morning.

Then, with a slap of the old screen door, we hurried back to the river. The sound of the spring stretching and then snapping back into place as the worn door hit the centuries-old jamb hung in the air until we were out into the water once more.

We stayed at Papa's Rock through the long summer and into the autumn, when on a fine, yet melancholy day towards the end of September, the potatoes were being clawed from their drills with hand diggers. (We measured the fishing seasons, beginning and ending, by the planting and harvesting of potatoes.) And the wide-soled runners of the drag-sled loaded with potato sacks made looping furrows in the freshly turned earth as an old horse hauled it toward our cellar bins. The tilled field with its rows of unearthed potatoes looked like a piece of Bible artwork in which peasants stooped to gather their crops to be carried in aprons to the house. I can remember when I noticed these real-life symbols for the first time; it was the day I had replaced my slingshot with a Daisy air rifle and my father allowed me to drive the new second-hand half-ton truck in the stubbled fields, while the grown-ups tossed the sheaves of oats into its high board rack.

I had reached the age when I secretly grieved the passing of another angling year, as by then each one appeared less rewarding, less exciting than the previous—or memories of the previous. There was less thrill in catching and holding a fish, less heroism shown from fishing friends, less praise from family.

And I mourned the loss of my older friends who had grown beyond that innocent river life, drifting away to hang out on the village streets. It seemed like spending time in town on the weekend was a must when one reached a certain age, and that too much river could hamper one's mental growth. I had seen the look of guilt in their half-apologetic, self-deprecatory expressions, as if they had grown tired of what they now regarded as childish things, or were being mocked by the older ones for not doing so. As if in their countrified worlds they should have felt a touch of shame for wanting to move on, even though they had reached the age when there were more exciting things to do on a Saturday night. For there were girls to pursue, futures to plan. I watched them go and tried to understand. Because I suspect, like their older siblings, they had become uneasy with so much time spent so unproductively and sought after a more serious lifestyle beyond the river, where they could, with the same commitment, become professionals in a range of occupations: artists, teachers, sailors, fishers, or business people.

Yes, leave before they had grown to hate the country they had been born and raised in—a place of more hard work than pleasures—leave while there was still some innocence in which to return down the road, when the past would no longer be a threat. Go with a clear conscience because they had worked hard all their young lives, and now the next oldest could take over their responsibilities and help keep the farm going. Yes, go on a one-way bus ticket with a loan from a finance company, co-signed by their parents, because they hadn't had a paying job to that point.

How dare you run out on us now, just when you've become of some use? their parents may have said when leaving the old home was mentioned; or I may have said this to my fishing pals. I was feeling the hollowness, not only of the lost company but also of a vanishing time and place where, because I was younger, that carefree innocence still lingered.

Still, when I look back, I don't think I ever felt completely alone on the river, so filled with life. As a nature lover, more and more, I actually preferred to be at one with the water, share in the river's soul. That I thought my chances of getting a fish were better if I didn't have to share the tackle was not a part of it, not in the least. I enjoyed the other's company, yes, and also sharing the rod because the bigger ones were better fishermen than me. As we were splitting our catch anyway, it doubled our chances and lessened the wading time. But it was not always about catching fish. The river meant more to me than just a place from which to get food for the dining-room table.

The river that ran through our community, its salmon angling and the camaraderie it offered to its children and youth, gave us a wealth of knowledge about life at all levels and the importance of meditation. As did the great elm trees, the gated lanes, and the hedge-fenced fields where wildflowers ripened under the burning August sun. As did the tree-shaded farmhouses and the velvety old barns with their thrashing doors propped open at haying time; the clumps of lilac and plum bush smothering our front doors that faced the river; the bird cherry that blossomed under the weathered windowsills of summer kitchens, with their wisps of woodsmoke and smell of warm bread; and the coolness of the well, where our grass-encircled reflections winked at us from under the water, cottony clouds in the background.

Nearby, a sunken footpath led down the hillside to the elm-treed interval where we played our cowboy games in spring, picked wild blueberries in summer, hunted partridge under the spectacular skies of autumn, and skated on the frozen river in wintertime.

These things we embroidered together to make the community's spirit whole. Combined, they offered a singular harmony that has long since become a place in my mind. In that old place and time, there was a youthful charm that only classical music can now express and which for me has stood up against the passing of the years. Just as the colour tones in a music score offer a composer's originality, these were subtle expressions, which, without some knowledge of the arts, I would never have been able to describe or experience again.

Perhaps it is briefly recalled in the scent of a lilac blossom when I'm walking down my city street, and for a moment I'm back there as a boy, walking over that landscape I so often gazed upon from Papa's Rock. And in that image, too, which becomes more elusive as time goes by, I find the same sensual pleasures, the same innocence, and the same youthful consciousness that existed on the home river. It's as though that old-world fragrance, more stable than my aging mind, has maintained its strong voice, and it carries in its smell the very best of old times.

I grasp and try to hold on to this river feeling in the same way that one might reach for the hands of an early love—protected from the years like a spring leaf that has been hidden between the pages of a Bible—and which, because of the moment it invokes, becomes more precious with the passing of time. It is as if one had to leave the river in order to grow, and then return, if only metaphorically, to realize what we had, as the landscapes and riverscapes so familiar to us in childhood were unseen. Perhaps that is why I struggled to leave the spot so long ago. I was there alone, quite alone toward the end, because, I now believe, I was more deeply rooted, more sensitive than most. For me there was not always a human tie so much as it was the place. I enjoyed more, yet suffered more, but hung on until that way of life was no longer real in the old-fashioned sense, in the same way that an ethereal affection resembles love only as the taste of strawberry ice cream is like that of the wild berry.

They say that a salmon river brings out the best and the worst in people, which I have witnessed in old homes and old communities. And I have watched people fight over lands and waters all my life. Maybe there was no love, just possession.

But there is nothing on this earth that does not end sooner or later. Nothing can be brought back to the ways of one's childhood, because somewhere along the way, innocence has been overtaken by ambition and growth, for better or for worse. The popular choice is to follow the main stream, so that all those early river memories become scattered like chaff in a wind. And all the philosophers, all the scientists, and all the environmentalists in the world cannot put it back together. Not the way it was.

From the Boat

"Anyone who at least once in his life has caught a perch or seen blackbirds migrating in the fall, when they rush in flocks over the village on clear, cool days, is no longer a townsman, and will be drawn towards freedom till his dying day."

Anton Chekhov, "Gooseberries"

The spring that I was twelve years old, my father built a boat. It was made of wide, rough boards, with a bow's knee that had been hewn from the root of a juniper tree. In April, when the days began to warm, he set up a workshop on the threshing floor of the barn, and then summoned my brothers and me to give a hand.

There, between the hay mow and the cow's stable, we placed two carpenter's benches five metres apart, and with a bucksaw and axe, set out to shape the long craft, separating the sideboards in the centre with wooden pegs set more than a metre apart and winching them into a curve, with a block and line, to join at the stern and bow. These boards slanted out slightly, like the sides of a clay flower pot, with the gunwales serving as a kind of rim. We chained the boards front and back so that the bottom crosspieces could be fitted together and nailed, their edges bevelled and sanded. We caulked the cracks with ropes of oakum by tapping them into place with a chisel and hammer, after which we covered the whole concern with a coat of rank-smelling hot tar. Three thwarts were added, and a seven-metre-long mooring chain was bolted to the bow with a granite rock wired to its end for an anchor.

When the boat was finished, in mid-May, we rolled her to the shore on poles and pushed her out onto the water, christening her *Verna*, after my late aunt, with a bottle of ginger ale. When the stern hit the water with a great splash, the boat almost capsized, and for a brief moment I wondered if she would float at all. But then *Verna* stabilized and set, high and majestic, a miniature version of the *Bluenose*—minus its masts, rigging, and canvas sails—tugging gently on the chain with each nudge from the passing currents. She did not set level however; the bow was canted slightly downward. And my father said this was because the juniper knee was less buoyant than the other lumber used. It was a subtle flaw, noticed only by those of us who helped in her construction, but it was a great lesson in boat building for us all.

Almost at once, kidney-shaped puddles started forming on the boat's bottom. These grew in size until the floor was completely covered with a centimetre of water.

"She's leaking like a basket!" I shouted. All spring long I had been looking forward to this day. I wanted to pole the boat out into the middle of the home pool, drop the anchor and cast a fishing line toward Jardine's Hole; I had seen salmon jumping out there. "Quick! Let's bail her out 'fore she sinks!"

"No, no," my father assured me. "After the boards soak awhile, they'll tighten up and she'll be okay."

Of course he was right. When the boat had been in the water for a few hours and the boards began to swell from the dampness, the cracks sealed themselves, the tar hardened, and she stopped leaking. We bailed her out with shovel-like motions of the paddle, and *Verna* remained dry inside thereafter.

Of all the things that my father did for my brothers, my sister, and me in those early days, building that vessel was the most important statement he could have made. Maybe this was because the boat came along at a time when I had reached the rebellious stage and wanted more than anything to break away from the family and be free; or maybe the craft was just a good form of conveyance that would get me to where the big fish lay, so that I could reach them with a cast. Whatever it was, the river—now with the boat added—had become a place to hang out. And I will be grateful to my father for this until my last dying breath.

On days of wind and sunshine, I would go to the shore, pole *Verna* out into the fast-flowing currents, and drop the anchor. The chain rattling over the gunwale could be heard for a long way on the water and sounded like a machine gun firing. I would lie on the boat's sun-warmed bottom, protected from the wind by the high, dory-like sideboards, and gaze upward to where a sunlit silver bullet made a chalk-like vapour trail across the sky, and let the ebb and flow of waves that lapped against the hull, those blue moving furrows of water, rock me to sleep. There were waves that came with the wind, and there were bigger swells that came in the cross-chop of passing motorboats. Both rolling surfs had an illusory value in that they changed the riverscape, transformed my leisure into alarm. I stayed low and hung on, feeling the spray of water that came in over the side and tossed the boat on the surface like a lily pad. Indeed, when the winds and the boats came together that way, I was grateful that the *Verna* was seaworthy, until the swells gradually diminished, along with the breezes and the trolling boats of the sport fishers, and the big river settled into crystals once again where the wind and sun touched it.

There were two winds at play out there. The upriver gusts were both warming and cooling, and would rock the boat like a cradle when the stern swung upstream, tugging gently on the chain that stretched crossways and downward in a belly—because the wind had relieved tension on the anchor—toward the gravel bottom, and which would snap the craft back into position when the chain tightened against the currents. And the land breeze, with the rain and sun in it, came in over the side boards from off the meadows and the woods, filled with the scent of field flowers and pitch, and reminded me of the ever-present aches and pains from the inland toil. These winds, which appeared to be duelling for supremacy, were tinged at once with a sense of freedom and obligation, the latter of which always surrendered to the boat and the old river's seductiveness.

There, anchored at midstream, was a place to contemplate and smell the drifting pollen releasing from shoreline shrubs—the lilac, the bird cherry, and the hawthorn blossom—sometimes mixing with the stench of a decaying shad that clung to a protruding branch in some upriver eddy, the fish-smelling boards, the tar and oakum, and tobacco smoke. There was also the underlying scent of the cough syrup I took for my asthma, plus the medicated ointment and Vaseline salve that my mother applied to my hands and lips when they became chapped from the wind and the water and the sun, and the Noxzema creams that were a cure-all for sunburn. All these blended together to create an odour that even today, when I'm around the river and old boats, reminds me of that early summer of my adolescence. All of this appears to have happened in the passing of one long season, but of course it was not that way at all: it was in fact between the years when I was eleven and fourteen.

The motorboats that passed by, oh so close, were sometimes driven by the innocent, teenaged river guides, smiling because they had found summer work on the river, their school days over. The tourists sitting upright and proper in the front seats, not knowing exactly what part of the river they had come from, or indeed where they were heading, were trusting the sober young employees to take them to places that would make their vacations memorable and give them a whiskey-enhanced reputation in their circle of anglers back home. These people from away always chuckled as they paused to take a photograph of our homemade boat—as though it were a piece of folk art—with me, a local lad, barefoot (we never wore shoes in the summertime), in cut-off pants, fishing with a bamboo pole and not the fibreglass rods like the sports were using. Some kind of Mark Twain character, I supposed.

And I felt a strong suspicion towards these people and their motives for being here. Were they just looking for fish? Or were they exploring the idea of purchasing property—for a tenth of its value—from a hard-luck relative. For in my own time, I had seen farms sold in our little settlement, their houses and fields abandoned, the community degraded to a destination for the foreign fishers and their cottages. The sports stayed on the river until they could no longer see the sun, except where it touched the tops of the trees and made windows blaze on the east side, and then it was gone into the black-treed horizon; time for everyone to get off the water.

This was the age when we, the river children, learned how to pole a boat. It was like milking a cow or weeding a vegetable garden, a necessary chore. The old people taught us to pole on the shallower starboard side and to steer by canting the pole this way or that while pushing from the inside, the same way that one might spin a golf ball from left or right with a simple move of the wrist, or lean into a pair of skates to make a quick turn and cut the figure eight. When poling, it was considered a disgrace to shift hand-holds, move the pole from one side to the other to control the direction, perhaps dropping water on the passenger and breaking an important stride, even losing ground in the process. Indeed, it was a great credit for a youngster to be regarded as a good boat person, and many of us who grew up on the river practised our skills daily. I doubt if there is a man or woman on this river today who can pole a boat against the strong current, empty or loaded with cargo, as my grandfather used to do with the log-driver's portage scows. It has become a lost art, except perhaps among the First Nations people, who make it a priority to hang onto their river traditions.

Because *Verna* was so long and heavier up front, she was always difficult for my young arms to navigate against the river's fickle ways, especially if I was fighting a strong, downriver breeze and unfavourable currents. She plowed the water when I was in the stern alone, and if there were someone sitting up front, paddling or rowing to help move things along, the boat became harder to push and almost impossible to steer. Still, that boat was used every day, either by the adults in a more practical way or by my brothers, sister, and me, even in showery or thundery weather, so intoxicated were we with the river and a sense of escape.

This was the boat that I held against the spring currents while my grandfather stood in the centre and, using an iron-banded, hardwood maul, drove the spruce pickets into the riverbed to set his ten-fathom gill net for the first runs of gaspereau. In mid-May these fish swam in schools upstream along our shore in water that was two metres deep. (Earlier in the spring, in the dooryard, I had held up the meshes for Papa as he simmed the net, using a handmade cedar fish needle and twine, half-hitching it, top and bottom, to the long tarred ropes, placing burnt cedar floats on the top line and wrapping pieces of chimney lead on the bottom.) The old man knew those fish were running at that time of the spring because, he said, they always came into the river when "the alder leaf was a mouse's ear."

After the net was set, my grandfather and his cronies reclined on a bench that was placed near the water's edge, under two upright, slanting poles covered with tarpaper, even on days when it was raining and there was a raw upriver wind. They smoked their pipes and talked of the old days and the many fish they had caught, the horses they had broken, and the dangerous log jams they had helped to unsnarl. When they saw the net floats bobbing and caught a glimpse of a fish's side flashing in the water, they jumped off that bench and pushed the boat out into the river to overhaul the net and take the sharp-bellied gaspereau from their gill-tangled holds. These fish covered the boat's bottom as they flounced and thrashed about, sounding like oak leaves flapping in a windstorm. Later, up in the little brook that ran past the barn, the gaspereau were scaled, gutted, and salted in wooden barrels, their heads left on so they could be hung on wires and smoked the following winter.

This was the boat that on moonlit October nights, my father and a neighbour poled upstream and let the boat drift down past home, with the tideway salmon net stretching across the water in a wavering curve, while they watched for a school of fish to entangle and be hauled in over the side. They did this until there was a half barrel of salmon salted in each of our homes.

Through the winter, generally on Fridays, my mother and grandmother soaked and boiled these fish to serve with half-peeled potatoes at suppertime. Or they made fish cakes. Once in a while the salmon were smoked, along with the gaspereau, in a small shack out back of the summer kitchen. And for the old men there was great concern about getting them done just right; sometimes, in conversation, they ate a whole fish raw, so tasty were they, with just the right amount of salt left in the fish to make us drink water, flush out our kidneys.

This was the boat that my brothers, sister, and I anchored in midstream, when the river was deserted during the dry season, and we swam from. We would dive off the stern and stay under the water a good long while, and then emerge to grab the bow and rock her up and down and make a great scudding sound, frightening the dragonflies that alighted on the gunwales, corrugating the water, and spooking the swallows that scooped down to pick insects off the moving surface. Sometimes, on days of strong upriver winds, we fashioned a sail from an old bedsheet or a canvas tent. Then we would get into the boat and let the water take us downstream to the wire bridge, where on the middle abutment, we hoisted the sail on a canoe pole, and using a paddle for a rudder, let the wind push us back up the river. Obsessed with virility, we would sing profane sea shanties as we went along.

In September, we paddled *Verna* across to the MacDonald place, an abandoned farm where we gathered wild crab apples for stewing. On the way back we ate a few apples in crossing and we tossed their sour cores upon the water for the rising chub to feed upon. For those trips, because our parents were in the boat and we wanted to show them our best behaviour, everyone sat on the thwarts while my brother Winston and I, sitting front and back, took the long arm-strokes that made little whirlpools spin behind the oars and caused the big salmon to make waves ahead of the boat as they hurried away from our intended course.

This was the boat that, in the summer of 1956, each morning my buddies and I poled to Taylor's Mountain, a kilometre upriver from home. Ralph Campbell, Harold's brother, or his half-brother Lloyd Sturgeon (sometimes both), would arrive at our door with a fishing rod, often in the first light before sunrise and long before I had eaten breakfast. In the ghostly fog, we hurried across fields of ripening grain and newly mown hay to the shore, where we took turns standing in the boat's stern with our feet braced like those of a boxer backed into the ring's ropes and leaned our full weight into the black spruce pole, while the other sat on the thwart nearest the middle and paddled. We made our way slowly against the currents, moving a bit faster in the slack water, staying as near as possible to the shore, while struggling to keep the boat moving forward in the heavy currents, where gravel bars had broken up the flow. At that time of the morning there were palm-sized chunks of foam like whipped cream adrift in the fast-moving waters. These crowded together in the channels and made moving shadows against a gilded bottom when the sun touched them. Everything was tranquil, as if it were a Sunday.

Oh, I wish I could more accurately describe the river dawns, the middays, and the sunsets and what feeling they stirred in me at that age. I wish I could tell you what I observed, as the first tint of dawn emerged from the night sky, making the water orange, brightening with the sounds of morning as the sun appeared over the tops of those old dark trees, climbed slowly against the sky, and transformed the maple-syrup-like water into crystal and then into ink, with the help of just a subtle breeze. Birds sang and trees sighed, touching me with their sounds and scents so that I could taste the coming day and knew it would be a good one. For things were always good at that time of the morning.

I wish I could tell you how those gradual changes from night to morning translated into dreams of the future and reflected a series of new horizons, new hopes for me and my river friends. I still wonder if these dreams of hope had anything to do with how I regarded myself back then, that because I grew up on the river and so far from town, I felt inferior to youth of the outside world, and tended to disparage my own ability, as farm boys do, even my existence. And that the morning's light brought with it a sense of confidence. Until my new-made plans of morning were overtaken by farm practicalities and through the difficult workdays were buried beneath the back-breaking endeavours of muscle and blood and sweat, and forgotten once more. Only to resurface when the dawn broke through again, for it is in a river child's nature to keep pushing forward, against the currents, against the odds, always pushing. Even now, so many years later, a morning sky on the water awakens in me a new kind of optimism.

"Yes, a place of dreams, that ol' river is," my father used to tell me. "But they are only dreams. And we have to struggle to make them happen, make them real."

Halfway to the mountain, just before we hit the strong waters of Bull's Run, we shifted positions and the one who was rested took over in the stern as boatman. As the pole bowed from the strain, ground into the gravel bottom, and tangled in the long undulating strands of eel grass—and might have snapped, sending the poler sprawling into the water—we forced the boat along while the white water plowed from beneath her bow. (These were the same shallows that chuckled in the night or on hollow mornings before a rain, creating the patches of drifting foam.) Then it was easy going again through the old slow-moving waters owned by the Clelands and the Bounds and on past the big submerged Johnston Rock that made the water gulp day and night, until we reached the Dunphy camp, a clapboard shack set in a grove of cedars at the foot of Taylor's

Mountain, and which faced the best salmon pool in that stretch of river. There we put the boat gently to shore, got out, and sat for a while. We shared a cigarette and watched the water for a rising fish before moving along in the shallows to the top of the pool.

This little river expedition we experienced every morning that summer—pole to the mountain and fish our way back. And I can still recall the indecent little rhymes we chanted along the way—"The Red Light Saloon" and "The North Atlantic Squadron":

> Here we come, full of rum,
> Looking for women to...

At the top of the Dunphy Pool, my fishing friend pushed the boat to centre stream, where I eased the anchor over the side into water two metres deep. And in so doing I could see my zigzagging reflection, the long, kinked arms in the water below, reflecting the shorter, straight arms above, hands—so near the water—exaggerated like the claws of lobsters.

We started working our way, one on a side, angling down through the pool. At first we made the short casts, just the leader and a metre of line. These became longer until we could reach no further. Of course, each cast had to be timed so our lines were not entangled with one another. When we figured we had covered the water on a given drop, we switched positions and each one tried the other side with another fly pattern, another presentation which brought his personality in relationship with the fish. We always angled with different fly-hook patterns, different strokes of the line, unless we discovered that the fish were rising for a given combination; then we used the successful one until the water's tint or temperatures changed.

When one of us hooked a fish, he would make his way to the head of the boat and fight the salmon, while the other stood in the stern—scoop net in hand—and watched as the fish took its long run, and the rising slant of the casting line became more shallow under the water, until the salmon jumped clear of the surface and fell heavily, sending a spray of crystal prisms into the air. We knew the weight of the fish by the height of this spray and by the fish's ability to hold deep because we had seen many and had fought many—big, bright sea-run fish too—caught by us and by our parents. We knew the fish was tiring when it started spending more time near the surface, showing its dorsal fin and the tip of its tail, until it was steered over the landing net and lifted into the boat and killed. We seldom went ashore to land a salmon, unless we didn't have enough line on the reel or we were holding up anglers who fished behind us in the pool.

When the missile-shaped salmon was boated, it thrashed against the planking until it was clubbed on the head and thrown up into the shade of the boat's bow, where its eyes grew lifeless like they were in a work of taxidermy. While each of these fish had its own fighting characteristics and brought with it its own adrenalin rush, we never individualized them as trophies, never demonized them as great fighters. Rather, we felt a sense of closeness toward them for their fighting spirits and gratitude toward the river gods for offering up this great dinner. We never weighed, measured, or photographed a fish, never held it out of the water while it gasped for breath; Papa said that showed disrespect for the species and that only non-river people did these things. And we were fishermen, not the tourists, who wore fancy clothes and used the big overkill equipment, who fished for bragging rights and the records they kept, and who held priorities so remote from ours. No, for us it was more than a sporting event, it was a fish for the supper table. It was also a chance to be at one with the river's offering, challenge the fish's pull to the bottom, feel its heart beat, taste its scales and blood which were so much a part of the rural soul. And we learned to love these fish because they were such an important part of our lives and our community. Even now the scent of fish in a market takes me back to that old place and time.

We continued angling in the same rotation until we felt we had covered the best water between Taylor's Mountain and home. We could divine where the salmon lies were and the presentations required to bring these fish to the boat. Sometimes, under the scorching midday sun, if we hooded our eyes, we could see the salmon—sensitive to changes in the wind or the sky's lightness and the very real threat imposed by the osprey and the eagle—where they took refuge in deep water, perhaps behind a submerged rock. From above the surface they looked slim and long, their tails stroking the water like soft, wide brushes. And we would cast for them, unsuccessfully, before moving on. As we knew, they had a lot of self-control and like an old love were not of easy virtue.

When we had drifted back to my father's farm at mid-afternoon, we fished the old home pool, before pushing the boat to shore and mooring her in the tall grass, tossing the anchor into the rushes where it may have spooked a meadow hen. Then we divided the catch and headed up the hill to arrive home in time for supper.

As we did these things, we sang the old boat shanty from my grandfather's day.

Fisherman's luck
Wet to the arse
And a hungry gut.

We were always hungry by that time of day. To me there was nothing on earth that could fuel an appetite like being on the river in any exposure: sun, wind, or rain. Everything was exaggerated out there, and time slipped by more quickly when we were on the water. We could lose track of the hours and life's turmoil that way, forget the rest of the world ever existed.

River Grass

I could tell it was haying time when I pulled on a strand of timothy and it would not come apart at the joint; rather, it came out of the ground, roots and all. Or when I saw the cat's cradles of fine-top or the raven nests of clover drifting downstream on the water. Metre-long blades of shore hay drifted past, too. These were not like the slimy strands of eel grass that twisted and turned under the water and stuck between my toes when I was wading, grasses that grew to the surface during the dog days of August to make floating strings of leafy garland. No, these were the long-stemmed, transparent flutes that emerged through the beach sand like swamp reeds among the fireplace boulders, and at the top of each one, a miniature tinselled Christmas tree. Their long, jagged leaves were as sharp as razor blades when I held them between my palms to make a whistle.

These grasses, canebrake high in places where the heron stood and the dragonfly teetered, if not cut from their scattered stubble and made into hay—for bedding under the cattle, or if the spring was late, as feed for the horses—turned a pale yellow in high summer and then a deep orange under the late August sun. In autumn, when the wind was up, these grasses blew in broad sweeping waves that rattled like dried cornstalks, offering a prairie-like ambiance that was genuinely deep-rooted, and because of the choppy dark waters that the grasses fringed upon, there was a touch of romance. These were the days when realtors sold the river properties, taking advantage of the grass and the water in constant motion under bright sunlight to make them appear more valuable than on a drab, calm day. As if it would be this way in all seasons and this was the best place in the world in which to live and fish. Or like the love stories we encountered in the movie house, in which there was always wind and water, sometimes even a bonfire that added to the scenery.

Nowadays, in the spring of the year, after the ice leaves the shores that are no longer mowed, these same long grasses lie in a downriver slant, as if the beaches were an endless straw mat, gold and dusty, and as decorative as a lace-trimmed cushion, as are the river's islands that were hayed annually and where our cattle sometimes grazed.

But when I was angling the home pool in the late Julys of my early teen years—when I was slim as a lath but almost as tall as my father—these shore grasses drifted past me, half submerged, like a crop of unravelled shredded wheat, having fallen from the racks of the big spoked, iron-soled wagons that teams of horses were hauling from the elm-treed islands, the ravines, and marshes just upriver from home.

At that time in July, the community smelled of hay. And the seed and the blossoms that floated on the water's surface, and which the fish sometimes rose for, appeared to be in competition with the artificial fly hook I presented over them. Strands of grass caught up in my leaders and hooks and made them skate and skip on the water to create long stringing wakes that trailed after my flies like many hungry eels. The grasses wrapped themselves like straw-tufted scarves or wigs of dirty-blond hair around the exposed rocks, lodged in my anchor rope, clogged up my pulley, and made life miserable for me when I was trying to catch a salmon for the dinner plate. These long grasses became entangled in the canoe poles of river guides and clogged the water intake valves of their outboard motors. And as if the grass had a mission to protect the salmon from all river people, it lodged in the meshes of poachers' set-nets to create wicker rugs that drifted away in the night.

To get to the island grass, the farmers had to wade through the river with horse machinery—the mowing machines, the rakers, and the heavy truck wagons—in places where the water was shallow, like at the head of rapids. And the hay loads hauled across these low-water bars to the big grey barns drooped down over the water-and-sun-faded wheels to look like the thatched roofs of English cottages. Some of this hay toppled into the water when an iron rim ground over a submerged rock—the sound could be heard for kilometres along the water—and the wagon tilted. Sometimes, too, a whole load was lost because the crossing was attempted when the water was on the rise. For sure, the islands and the shores were not easy places to harvest a crop from. But these areas, so full of wildlife, were always mowed, from the high-water mark to the riverbed, the entire length of the waterfront on each farm. It was not until that way of life ended in the early 1960s—due to government's social programs and because farm products could be purchased at a supermarket for less money than they could be raised at home—that a growth of dogwood, alder, and poplar took over those rich bottomlands.

Our shore, because of its steep inclines and the ruggedness of bush and boulder, had to be mowed with a scythe. And I can well remember the many long hours of walking behind my grandfather, ten feet tall, as he hand-mowed the shore as well as the little brooks, which by that time in the summer had partially dried up so that they were moist and soggy under my bare feet. Papa always did this in the early mornings when the dampness in the grass made his long blade crop the better. He left a latticework of slain bulrushes while keeping his sharp blade canted slightly upward above the rocks and the exposed shrub roots. His mechanical stride was uniform as he swung the scythe, each swath raking aside the last one's fallen shrubbery. Sometimes he stopped, shook his handkerchief, wiped his brow and then fanned himself against the mirages of the heat, the attack of mosquitoes.

Mindful not to bruise my feet on stubble, or step in the white, foamy grasshopper spittle, the cocoons of cotton batten that stuck to the low dead limbs, or the spider's night webs—often you must have seen them while walking in the morning grass—that hung in the undergrowth like agglomerations of old lace, I lifted the black alder and the red dogwood branches so the old man could mow under them. Bent by the ice jams, these heavy stalks arched upwards and bowed sharply to the ground in a downriver curve, like water squirted from a fountain or birch trees weighted down from an ice storm. In the words from Robert Frost's "Birches": "once they are bowed / So low for long, they never right themselves." These bigger shrubs—rank-smelling and which cast arching brown shadows upon the stubble shore—were never cut down, not here, where their roots kept the riverbank safe from erosion. But Papa would chase an alder shoot into a cedar swamp to keep the pressing trees from overtaking our fields. Yes, there were things to cut down, and things not to cut down. It depended upon what they stood for.

And I can remember the clanging of my grandfather's scythe stone as he slapped the steel blade to give it an edge. With the end of its crooked handle firmly planted into the ground, he closed an eye and took sight along its decreasing, curved rapier, which rang with a different note the further out he reached, in the same way that a church bell peals clearly in a hazy summer's calm and then more shallow when the wind is up. As if, like the schoolhouse bell or the intermittent chapel's knell, he had done this to summon me there. For I had heard him from the house and felt obligated to run, give a hand. He summons me there even now. For these places and times live only in the minds of those who have experienced them, and have long since vanished in a wilderness of new growth and modernization.

And the steady, monotonous tones of the crickets, the hum of bees in the summer's bloom were further musical notes anyone in the community could have heard from that shore. Plus the sour taste of the half-green berries I sampled while helping Papa with the haying: I still relate the two, the twang of the scythe stone and the tang of the berries.

The sounds were contrasted only by the bittern that lived in the tall grass at our shore. This bird made earthly sounds that resembled a piledriver in motion. And the scent of the water thereabouts carried the symbolic taste of fresh salmon.

"And I'll never see my Nelly anymore," Papa sang when the mowing was finished, and then he hung the scythe on a limb of a big spruce tree, high out of reach from the little ones.

Later, with a wooden rake that had a rack of wire rings and a hand-whittled tooth, I gathered the fallen rushes and carried them from the shade of the tall bank trees to be scattered near the water's edge, where they would ripen under the afternoon sun. I would return that evening with a pitchfork and bunch the hay into ricks so it could more easily be tossed into the rung-rack as the big wagon moved along the rocky riverbed and the droop-headed horses nuzzled at the water that flowed between their hooves as it trickled slowly towards the sea. They lifted their heads only when the reins were tightened, setting themselves to haul the crop up the steep hill to be pitched into the mows of our threshing barns.

In the heat of summer, this was hard work for a small lad who was suffering from hay fever, which made my eyes water and kept me sneezing, gasping for breath, sneezing, a condition my father and grandfather thought I was faking to get out of work. I remember Papa singing my praises irrepressibly to keep me moving along, despite the anguish. (For the scythe and wooden hay rake, farm implements from his time, had by then become my boyhood enemies.) To me back then, these laborious old traditions represented expressions devoid of common sense, advancement by digression; pushing forward in an old-fashioned way while really going backwards with no illusions or expectations of anything better to come. Still, I kept my nose to the ground because I knew this fodder—some of which was burdock, nettles, and wild lupine—could be used for bedding, and God forbid, to feed the animals through the tail end of the long winter ahead, a time when the cattle had to be stall-fed, sometimes into late spring, before the pastures and the shores had started to green once more. Sometimes when we ran out of hay a cow or calf had to be sold.

But I now believe that my grandfather, and my father who followed so closely in his footsteps, hayed the shores more to keep their farm groomed than for any crop the labour may have produced.

"There's a disgrace people bring on themselves by living in a place where things are let go to hell," Papa said. "A fool has no conscience. And he always outlives his own legacy." He added, "And if ya live the right way lad, you'll go ta Heaven when ya die."

"But how do ya know, Papa?"

"I know. Don't ask me. I know. It's in the Bible. Forty days after ya die... the soul goes to Heaven. Until then it stays around home here. I've heard them at the door—your great-grandfather—yes, and in the attic the first few days after he died, and then in the pantry and the stovepipes. I heard him."

"But?"

"But ya gotta believe!"

Sometimes Papa would work himself into a frenzy about the government, which he felt was ruining our country. He said that the only difference between a Conservative and a

Liberal was that a Conservative prayed in public and drank in private, whereas a Liberal drank in public and prayed in private. He claimed he could tell who was who, on sight, because the Conservative was always clean-shaven and better dressed. And when it came to doing business with people Papa said that, for his part, he would rather deal with an optimistic atheist than a pessimistic Christian.

Sometimes, after the hay was cut, my grandfather made a flute by cutting holes a finger's distance apart in a swamp reed. Another summer tradition. And he played a little tune, "Danny Boy," sitting in his hall rocker while supper was being prepared. This was a far better sound than the cries of his old concertina, which he played on Sundays, "Onward Christian Soldiers." Papa was anything but a musician and had few, if any, artistic inclinations. Of course there were no masters here—I would not have been able to distinguish Chopin from Bach—rather, we were people learning to master ourselves, to exercise self-control.

Still, I wondered if my grandfather had been exposed early on to things different than woods, fields, and river, if he'd have been an influence—like his sister Marguerite who left the river as a teenager and performed as a dialect reader at Carnegie Hall in October of 1910—in the outside world. Had he been able to satisfy his life's ambitions, was he happy with his station in life, the internal rewards of owning a well-groomed farm? I think so. And yes, it meant as much if not more to him. A question of priorities.

In those days, my family and the river were my only real

loves. And there was nothing for me but contentment in both. It was a time before girls and sex and the love of these had entered my mind, a time before proms and dates, and going to the village on weekends to look for a better life. I guess you could say they were the days before my summer had really begun. While I was approaching the age when I would have had an interest in cars and motorbikes and fancy clothes, perhaps even a lover, until then, all such ambitions had been kept smothered by the lure of the country and river, my own silent pleasures. I observed the bonfires that smoked on the treeless hills of a Saturday morning's cowboy game; I strolled the homely country lanes that divided the pasture land from the furrows of plowed field that had laid open the strong-scented earth like the pages of a book; climbed the rank-smelling oak trees that creaked in the wind; drank up the meditative silences of the woods, brooks, and river; and reclined to rest on the scorching gravel bars under a cloudless sky.

It would be a long time before I grew away from these simple pleasures and moved into the outside world only to eventually realize that true happiness lay not in the discovery of truth but in the search for it. And that maturity—which should have fostered happiness—had no solid beginning and certainly no romantic ending, that dreams became real only in fairy tales. By that time my grandfather was an old man in sweat-stained suspenders and a frayed straw hat, with his flannel shirt sleeves rolled up to his elbows. But like Ulysses, he still carried inside him the unquenched fires and the dangerous spirit of his youth. While time had ravaged him with a mental and physical weakening, together with a network of fine wrinkles and a tussle of white hair, he had hung on to his robust temper, his nobility of soul, and his love for the land. He never lost those.

My adoration for him now overshadows any failings he might have had. Nor did our conflicts inspire any long-term indifference. Decades after his death, he continues to exercise his influence as I recreate through memory or imagination the happiness of those early years, though work-laden and disciplined, more precious than a piece of silver.

I know that my grandfather was well respected on the river, too, because when he died at the age of ninety-one, people from miles around home came to our farmhouse to pay their respects.

Papa told me many times that it was "the little things in life" that separated greatness from mediocrity, set the traditionalists apart from those who would not waste their time mowing a shore or a swamp, maintaining a fence, or pruning an apple tree; people who lived insensible to such trivial things as a well-groomed piece of property. He told me that time was always the best measuring stick when it came to success, however humble; and the pride of doing the little things successfully demanded a certain respect from the river's community, and these were the best rewards.

I now believe this to be true. For why else would I be writing this essay, so many years later? It is these little things that now take me back there. As Anton Chekhov's narrator observes in "A Boring Story from an Old Man's Notes," "Only one who loves can remember so well."

The Wire Bridge

The community in which I was born and raised consisted of a dozen wilderness farms, which extended on both sides of the river for two kilometres each way from the bridge. On our side there was a one-room school, a church, a church hall (where we went to movies and chicken suppers), a post office, a CNR train station, and my father's general store. To get to these establishments in winter, those who lived on the other side travelled across on the ice, but in the spring, summer, and fall, the two solitudes were joined together by a wire bridge.

For me, as a five-year-old child, walking that shaky span for the first time was a frightening experience. And I can remember my mother telling me, "Don't look down! Stare at the trees on the other side." I clutched her coattails and moved along with a foot-dragging fearfulness. At that age, before my school days had begun, even the sight of that swinging bridge frightened me, and I had nightmares of falling through its wire structure into the dark moving waters, so far below. But as I grew older, the bridge crossings became as commonplace as strolling along the gravel highway or walking a rail on the train tracks, and I was assured by the older kids, and my parents, that because of the bridge's sturdiness it was just as safe. That old cable bridge, though crude in structure, held a prominent place in my boyhood, and in the survival of our little community of Keenan.

On each riverbank, the bridge's abutment was a rectangular cribwork of aged cedar and fieldstone that could be seen from a long way off. The abutments stood against the elements like weather-beaten hovels, their log walls chinked with rock and sprouting greenery. On top of these pillars there were slabs of concrete wherein four railway rails were sunk to hold the steel cables that hung like a barrel-stave hammock across the water. These cables were enclosed with a page-wire railing. Hardwood two-by-fours were wired to the bottom strands at one-metre intervals to make it look from a distance like a rope ladder. Two boards nailed to these crosspieces made the pedestrian walkway. On top of each abutment there was also a railing of cedar posts and pig wire, which made it resemble a balcony or a widow's walk, and there was a long set of steps with wood banisters that descended to the ground. From there, a crooked and sunken footpath coursed the elm-treed intervals and on up the hills on each side to where our farmhouses stood.

That old swinging bridge must have been two hundred metres long; it sagged down toward the water at midstream and up again to the opposite abutment. Often, during the spring runoff, the lowest part of the bridge was caught in the flow. It tossed about and was pulled into the heavy currents, which stretched the cables and filled the mesh railings with brown grass and sticks. I can remember lying in my bed on an April night and listening to the mournful freshet sounds, the boards slapping against the water, which seemed louder in the darkness, as the lumber creaked and the cables groaned while they caught and held, for a moment, the trees and old buildings that came drifting down the river. And I wondered if the bridge would survive until morning.

After the runoff, the structure looked like a lopsided, straw-woven hall runner hung out to dry in the sun and breeze. The upriver winds, which created whitecaps on the black rolling water below, made the bridge flap like a clothesline, and I was not permitted to go on it until the government inspectors came to winch up the cables and tighten the clamps, so the men of the community could free the page wire of its brown grass and sticks and make the whole concern safe for crossing once more.

As children, my brothers, my sister, and I, as well as other youngsters of the community, learned to walk the bridge, even in windstorms, when it was bouncing about at centre stream, where the cables appeared more slack and the upriver wind got a good rake on the structure. For a youngster in grade four or five, it was a nerve-testing experience to be out there when those gales tossed me against the railings, made the legs of my trousers flap and my open shirt belly like a sail. I can remember getting seasick at midstream, lying down, closing my eyes, and praying for those windswept hours to pass. When this didn't happen in a matter of fifteen or twenty minutes, between gusts I crawled on all fours back to our side. Crossing that bridge in a gale was something all of us river children had to learn to do. It was like poling a boat, milking a cow, or hoeing a vegetable garden.

When we were a little bigger, and when it was calm, we ran the bridge with our bicycles, gliding down our side to gain speed and climbing to the opposite abutment, where we braked quickly, leaving black skid marks on the cement like a jet plane stopping on an aircraft carrier. And the breezes blew the red, white, and blue plastic ribbons we had fixed to the ends of our handlebars. Biking on the bridge was risky, as the seats of our bicycles were higher than the top cables and a gust of wind could have pushed us over, which would have been fatal. More daring still was when one of the older lads crossed on his Wizard, a small motorcycle popular in the early fifties. Sometimes, when the wind was up, we just lay on the boards at centre stream and smoked cigarettes we had rolled ourselves with dried-out makins and a book of papers, let the bridge rock us as though we were in a cradle, while the scent of salt water and decaying algae blew up the river from the distant sea.

For sure, when it came to flirting with danger, the bridge held a kind of magic for us all, and trying to out-do one another, we pushed our stunts to the limits and beyond. For excitement, when there was an upriver wind, once we tried to frighten one of the adults who happened to be walking the bridge. We waited in the bushes until he reached midstream, then we stole out on the bridge a ways and bounced ourselves on the boards, which made the cables shimmy and gave him hand-numbing shocks like those we got from our pastures' electric fences. The reaction carried along the cables in waves as we yanked the top lines hard to make them slap our victim, so that his movements became a series of starts and stops as he crouched, held on, then stood on shaky legs to stagger forward. His clothes flapped like a windblown scarecrow's, and his twisted shadow danced on the water below like a crane in a minefield, until he eventually got down and crawled on all fours. Then, before he made it to our side, we ran and hid in the trees, while he shook his fist and cursed at us, saying that he was going to tell our parents.

Because of a severe scolding from our teacher and parents —"Don't shake the bridge when the adults are crossing!"—this stunt never happened again.

When we were a little older the bridge became a place for us to congregate: to fish, swim, bike, or just hang out. Like a magnet, it drew us there in the same way that a diner with a jukebox and a soda fountain might have attracted the town-bred youth. We went to the bridge on Saturday nights and did stunts with our bikes. Some of us dived over the side into a deep hole, gained the water's surface, and swam hard, letting the currents carry us down and into shore, only to drag ourselves back onto the grass like some amphibious creature and walk back along the warming sunlit fields to the steps, where we waited in line to dive again. And as we waited, we smoked cigarettes with the lit ends inside our mouths, just as our uncles had done when they were "overseas." The girls of the community, my sister among them, played these dangerous games with us.

From late spring through to the fall, up on that bridge we could see the river's bottom for a long way around us, like a field of tiny brown pebbles under glass. You could say that we had a kingfisher's view of the river's species as we watched the various schools of fish swim under us on their way upriver to spawn. We threw rocks to scare the gaspereau into a net that our fathers and grandfathers had hung from pickets near the shore, so that they could get a few of these fish for smoking.

Or perhaps we'd stand on the bridge with our fishing lines in the water in an attempt to jig a shad for the supper table. In the spring of the year, we hooked black salmon while walking back and forth and letting our long lines with buck-tail streamers swing across on the water's surface. When we saw a fish give chase and felt the big pull from below, we set the hook and ran to the nearest abutment, down the steps and along the shore, while reeling in line to swing the metre-long fish to our side, until we got it cornered in a big eddy, which we called the Dead Man's Hole, where the fish grew tired so that we could grab it by the tail and lift it from the water.

We knew it was illegal to angle from the bridge. Still, since we were crossing the river anyway (as we told the wardens) and were not impeding the passage of pedestrians, what was the harm in it? So they let it happen as long as we kept walking. And we could watch those big fish coming after our streamers for a good long way.

Sometimes we'd see bright salmon lying in the shade of the bridge, but from our vantage point it was impossible to get a fly hook to swing over them. One of us went upriver and waded out, while the others, up on the spans, directed a cast to where the fish lay. In that way we could see if the salmon made any move at all toward the fly that was being presented. It was here

I learned that a fly hook had to swing at just the right angle and speed before a salmon would make a move for it. A few centimetres too long or too short, a few kilometres per hour too fast or too slow just would not do.

It was fun to look down and see the underwater action, the movements the salmon made after each cast, things that would have gone unnoticed if you could not see the bottom. Sometimes it would be nothing more than a hurried waggle of the fish's tail; at other times, when the fly hook swung, the fish would move partway to the surface, then appear to change its mind and settle back; and if it did rise all the way, it was interesting to see how it made a complete turnabout before settling back to its resting place. If the fish took the fly and realized it was hooked and in trouble, it would head downstream fast, pointing its nose into the gravel bottom here and there in an attempt to pry the hook loose. (My father told me many times that a stressed or wounded salmon would always head towards salt water.) Of course most of the time these fish, especially the big ones, would not move for a fly, regardless of how and where it was cast—not in that twenty-plus-degree summer water. They would lie at an underwater spring, we suspected, or perhaps behind a teakettle-sized rock on the otherwise flat, pebbly bottom.

In an attempt to hold more salmon under the bridge, we carried rocks of that same size and dropped them over the top cable. We wanted to make the water turbulent, create more oxygen for the salmon to breathe, but for some reason this did not work, and the fish continued to lie behind the original stones. We dropped more rocks to make a kind of reef, and then the salmon did not lie in that place anymore.

However, these were ill-conceived efforts that time would cure. The rocks we had thrown into the river soon became buried in the gravel, and the bottom was smooth again. Later, my father told me that we should not have tried to improve the salmon's holding areas or to mess with nature; these fish were far too sensitive to be controlled in a simple way, and the stones had been a part of the natural riverscape for a zillion years. He said that adding something new that was not camouflaged with the river's bottom, or in sequence with the other stones, was more of an obstruction than anything—like trying to show a robin where and how to build its nest. It was a lesson for me never to fool around with the salmon's environment or other natural habitats.

Sometimes we'd see the lampreys, their big open mouths with many rows of needle-sharp teeth and great suction lips. These fish died in early summer and drifted downstream, sinking in the eddies or clinging to shoreline bushes like discarded, white nylon stockings. Once, I saw a lamprey clamped to the side of a salmon, attempting, I supposed, to suck its blood. I actually caught a salmon with a dying lamprey attached to its belly, and I had to pry the eel free with my jackknife. I wondered afterwards about the struggles that our salmon stocks had to go through in order to return to their spawning beds, some inflicted by us youth just approaching our mid-teens out there on the wire bridge.

I remember with affection the night of my junior prom, walking my date in the early hours of the morning across that old bridge and up the flat on the far side, a kilometre to her home. We stopped on the bridge at centre stream to sit, hold hands, and look at the galaxy of stars above us, their reflections in the water below. As we sat close, with our feet hanging over the side, and watched for a shooting star to wish upon, the big river below was silvered by the moonlight, and the trees along the shores, so silent and still, made piercing blue shadows like ghosts extending out into the water. With the sounds of toads singing along the shores, the laugh-like cry of the loons, and the scent of lilac and hawthorn blossom on a night in May, it was the most romantic place on earth. Almost divine.

I distinctly remember my date's silky black hair—with a cluster of potato blossom at the side—and her dark eyes, so kind and beautiful; she might have been a character from out of the *Arabian Nights*. And in her lightness of heart, my new-found love—though I had known her all my young life, as we had grown up with only the river separating our farms—sang that sentimental old school-closing hymn, "Now Is the Hour." It was an artistic side of her I hadn't noticed before, and I remember wondering if she was sensitive enough to have directed the messages in those lyrics as she rendered them, "Soon you'll be sailing far across the sea…You'll find me waiting here" toward me? So unsure of myself, I was looking to read something positive into each simple gesture she made. And she appeared to be in no hurry to go home. It was as if neither of us wanted to leave the bridge, which was a kind of neutral ground. Here we felt free from the parental anguish—from both shores—about our relationship, which we knew our families would think was premature, because we were too young to be involved with one another.

"I love you," she said. Words I believed, yet did not believe.

"I love you, too," I said. But I was not exactly sure of the depth of this phrase, the true implications of what the words really stood for. For sure, they seemed like the right words at the time, as they conveyed the height of emotions I was feeling just then.

In truth, I was trying not to love her. But it was like I couldn't stop what was happening, even though I could feel, down deep, it was going to be the most beautiful, yet most painful experience I would ever have.

"Will you take me home now in that new convertible of yours, bad boy?" she asked finally, when the first light of dawn appeared. We had taken off our stiff dress shoes and were making our way along on the bridge barefoot, she in a knee-length, white dress with the pink carnation I had given her the night before and I in a white sports coat and black slacks, popular fashions of the time.

"Yes, it's parked right over there on the flat. Can't you see its chrome glittering in the moonlight?"

"We'll be the envy of all the Blackville kids when we drive past the Ross Canteen with the top down, on the morning after the prom." Her eyes became challenging, as though, for the moment, she was sharing my secret longing to be with her forever and always. It was a radiance, somewhat remote yet real, and one that I have looked for in a hundred women since but never saw again, not with that same inner magnetism. Of course, neither of us was ever that same person again: controlled just then by our hormones, the growing pains of self-discovery.

"I certainly will be, with you beside me," I said and squeezed her hand. Then we stopped and kissed for what seemed like a long time. It was a kiss that still carries a special place in my heart, the drama of first love. It was not so much this young woman, but the state of mind she aroused in me, the anxious side of my own young soul experiencing emotions that were all so new and challenging. And suddenly I loved her like I had never loved anyone outside the family. For a brief moment her folks became my folks.

But I would not rest easy for a long time; lacking confidence, I feared what the future would bring because I could give only my love, and was not at all sure of her side of things, how deep her feelings really were for me, how committed she was to the relationship. So I kept these feelings hidden—as country youth will—and tried to enjoy the moment.

Of course there was no convertible. And there never would be. Our little dialogue was nothing more than a fiction we were acting out in our partnership of dreams. And because I could not give her a night of driving around the village in a convertible for all her classmates to see, and that she had to fake such things, saddened me. I wished I could have metamorphosed into the prince she was pretending I was, the one she deserved and would no doubt find in her travels. Because she was a princess, one who was seeking a life beyond our little community in bigger and higher places.

As the day broke clear, and roosters crowed, we left the bridge and followed the cow paths across the flat, through the misty pasture, and up the hill to her place. The fresh morning air was alive with the scent of blossoms, the voices of songbirds, and the peeping swamp sounds, which I had so often listened to from my bedroom window in the early mornings, and which would bring back this special time for years to come. The country was full of basic promise, early season assurances of a bright future. And love. Along the way, there were cattle gates to help each other over, rustic benches in the shadows of trees where we could sit and kiss awhile, and water troughs, where sleepy-eyed horses drank while swatting flies with their tails.

We met three women who were wearing hats and veils and who were obviously walking to early Mass at Our Lady of Mount Carmel Shrine in Howard. (For we were well into May, the month of Mary.) They passed without speaking to us, but we could hear their distant mumbling, their sighs of disgust. Then we heard the first bell, echoing along the water. I thought of my mother who had taught me the catechism and the Apostles' Creed, and I wondered what she would say to me when I got home after being out all night. And I felt a touch of guilt for how I had behaved. This was quickly overpowered by the events of the morning, the fact that I had my first love walking there beside me, step by step.

Wind chimes rattled in the ivy of my date's father's veranda, a signal to those inside that I had brought her home. Finally.

When I kissed her "goodnight" she said, "Wanna come into the veranda for a glass of champagne and some caviar?"

The bridge and the countryside where we hung out that night and morning was a place literally and spiritually dear to my heart, a kind of Eden. I left her house and walked toward home with a feeling of pride and a new sense of who I was, and what I would strive to become. It was an intoxication that I have never experienced before or since. As I approached the place on the cable bridge where we had sat for so long, her spirit was still alive in the scent of the rusty wires, the sun-dried boards, and the water, distinct feelings from affections that to me, just then, appeared as shaky as the old bridge itself.

Later in my bed, holding a pillow like the young woman in my arms, I dreamed of her. These were not dreams I could tell anyone about, either before or after breakfast, to make them come true, even though, according to Papa, all dreams that were told before breakfast had a better chance of becoming real. These dreams were an intoxicated reliving of the feelings that were greater than the real person and the occasion, however beautiful, could have ever lived up to. Yet the more I fantasized about her, the more beautiful she became, until my dream woman had far surpassed the young girl I had grown up with, and with whom I should have been on equal footing. So I told my family a bit of what had actually happened but kept the dream sequence deep inside, secretly tossing grains of salt over my left shoulder both to avert bad luck and in the hopes of making those dreams real. Still, I could not get up the courage to call her. Instead, I carried her love, or perceived love, inside me and waited for her to make the move, until there was nothing left to wait for and her presence was little more than a shadow on the water or a ghost in the trees.

She vanished from my dreams completely after I saw her in the village, sitting next to a guy in a red convertible, just as she had fantasized about doing with me on prom night. It was then I felt my first real burning of true jealousy. After that I could never see her as quite the same true love, in real life or in dreams, even though she had the most sensitive eyes and the most beautiful laugh in this world. It was as if I had known all along that she was beyond my reach, and so I felt a necessity to protect myself from any further hurt. But I prayed that the angels of the Lord would always look after her.

Looking back, I can now see that no love could have survived with so little real nourishment. In my own conceit, I had never given her any motivation to love me or any reason for her to believe that I loved her, rather the opposite. I held the silence of an overconfident suitor, while in truth I was broken-hearted. Just like one's youth, a first love once lost can never be reclaimed the same as before, and I accepted this with a fatalism filled with eternal desires, external regrets, a condition for which there might be a treatment, but certainly no cure.

After so many years, the emotional turbulence from that young love still flashes in my memory. And the wire bridge hangs as a kind of memorial to that unstable time of young love.

I still wonder if she found happiness beyond what—I am still so uncertain—I could have given her. I hope she did.

For I loved her too much to hold her back, interfere with her chances of achieving greatness.

I know that she married someone from the river, moved away and raised two daughters—who I am told look just like her—before she died of an aneurism in her mid-thirties. "She was the woman of my dreams," I told my father when he informed me of her sudden death.

And so she remains my dream woman, and forever young.

By the late seventies, more and more frequently the bridge was being damaged and sometimes even swept away by the spring waters. This was perhaps from the effects of over-grazing in the woodlands or climate change or both, which made the river increasingly inconsistent in its spring flows. Each time it was knocked down, it took longer to be repaired. And just as quickly that old way of life was being diluted by the new world order. Already our schoolhouse had been torn down, and children were being bussed to the big regional institutions in the city. The post office had been done away with and the railway trains had stopped running, their rusty tracks in the process of being dismantled. My father closed his store because so many of us young people had moved away to find work. Certainly there was no place in the modern day for something as shaky and impermanent as the wire bridge.

I had been away to live in the city for years, had married, and returned to the river—I suppose for nostalgic reasons—to find work and raise my family. I wanted my sons to know as

I did the country I had grown up in. On an evening in May, for old time's sake, I went over the river to fish the eddy for spring salmon as I had done so often as a boy. There had been heavy rains and the water was less than a metre from the bridge and rising. But there was no wind; the cables were steady. My son Jeff was with me and I can remember holding his hand, as my mother had held mine, while we made our way across, periodically glancing upriver for drifting objects that could catch in the wires and throw us into the big river. When I think of this now, I am sorry that I ever exposed my seven-year-old son to such a risk. But having grown up playing on the bridge myself, it never occurred to me then that we were in any danger. We fished until almost dark and made our way back across, safely.

The next morning the bridge was gone. Only the abutments remained. They stood on either side of the water like monuments to that old-world community. And the many great emotions it had brought to its children, gone.

At Rum Rock

If you were canoeing along that stretch of the river, you wouldn't even notice the boils, so subtle were they you'd have to crouch low to the surface, perhaps from downstream, before you could even detect the delicate embroidery set spinning by the underwater currents. And there was no gravel beach or exposed shoreline to help identify the place as a salmon holding pool. Along that shore the wild rushes grew tall and untrammelled, the path a vague parting in the grass. In fact, many less observant anglers, or folks from away, paddled right through the area, oblivious to its potential. And if, by chance, they stopped to fish, they'd have been instructed by one of the locals to wade into the pool (or not, depending on the height of the water), just in front of that birch stub or perhaps the big pine tree, back a ways on the riverbank. The water was leaden, melancholy and dark, and considered "non-fishable" by novice, fast-water fisher people, anglers who relied on the water's speed to straighten their forecast, swing their flies, and enhance their presentations.

Rum Rock, the place's namesake, was at the water level when the pool was fishing at its finest. From there looking upstream, one could see Taylor's Mountain, a small green summit with a quaint log cabin sitting on its foothill riverbank. Downriver, in the far bend, a white clapboard farmhouse, once so common in these parts, stood on a hillside. Around this house some draft horses kept the lawn.

This was the shore, including its riparian rights that in the early fifties my uncle traded (in small part) for a '48 Dodge half-ton truck, a vehicle badly needed around home at the time. It went, along with the abandoned farmlands and hillocks of lumber woods, to a car dealer, who as far as I know, never fished the pool. That owner eventually sold it to an American, who built a cabin beneath the pine tree and used the place to host barbecues and catch spring salmon. It was said that the new proprietor loved the pine tree and the grounds more than he did the pool; then his camp went adrift in an ice jam and he sold the property to a local businessman, a long-time friend and a schoolmate, who knows the history of the place. He shares it generously with my family and friends, giving us exclusive fishing rights.

Through the years, Rum Rock remained open for fly-fishing to my family and the ghosts of our old-name river lineage because we had once owned the place. This birthright was never challenged by other anglers or even other owners due to the pool's lack of potential—or supposed lack of potential—so our family tradition has been kept alive to this day.

In recent years, however, this patrimony is being poached upon by cottage owners who are not true river people and show no respect for tradition or etiquette, or for the value of solitude, which is being shattered far too often. They anchor their unfriendly aluminum motorboats in the run, boast about their catches, and cut us off in the cast, a condition my father called "new money."

But during the sixties and early seventies, my family fished the Rum Rock Pool extensively, and almost exclusively. Of course, we had fished bigger and better waters in the fifties, when my father was an outfitter here on the Miramichi and had log cabins "to let" near our home, which remain family cottages to this day. You might say that in those times the whole river was ours for the angling. Few of the locals fly-fished, so most pools were vacant, even when the big salmon runs were on.

As the sport of salmon angling gained popularity, more and more of our community's fishing waters became overcrowded, and many were sold to non-resident anglers, who were quick to put up "No Trespassing" signs in an attempt to eliminate the locals from the river. While through this time my family had maintained our home pool, Rum Rock was the place we went to fish after the Saturday and Sunday evening potluck meals that were weekly traditions at my parents' farmhouse. It was the atmosphere we went there for.

We poled the canvas canoes (Chestnut, Miller, or Sharpe), with the greatest of skills, from our shore, downriver, avoiding the shallows and giving in to the stronger currents. We moored at the head of a small eddy just upstream from Rum Rock, a white boulder shaped like the back of a giant pig and which by midsummer was partly hidden by the shoreline rushes. We sat on the rock and faced a sweltering sun as it sank slowly into the trees on the north side and which made spoke-like shadows that stretched across the river. And we cooled our feet in the water as we sipped our remaining heels of rum and after-dinner liquors and watched for a salmon to rise. In fact, the rock got its name from those very outings.

We also went there in the mornings, poling those same high-riding and silent boats close to shore where the trees kept the river shaded on our side. Patches of froth the size of playing cards—condensation from the night's dew—drifted downstream and did not evaporate until almost noon. The pool fished well at nine in the morning when the sun first touched the water, and again at eleven when the air and water temperatures equalized and the foam started to disappear.

Because of the invisible underwater currents, with perhaps a few bottom-fed springs, and the lack of a defined holding area, we had learned how to angle this water through trial and error. Experience and memory told us where the fish held, the angle of cast that was required, the speed of the hand action that was needed in the retrieve, and the kinds of slow-water fly patterns that were most effective, depending on the conditions and the state of mind the fish were in. For we had learned to think like salmon, to give them what they wanted and when, as one might try to appease an old love whose favour he is looking to regain.

The pool fished better in the higher water of June and early July, as the low oxygen content left it stagnant in the dog days of August, except perhaps after a rain. It fished better still in the fall months when those big, spawn-laden fish tended to seek the deeper and more slow-moving waters. In fact, so consistent were the lies when the conditions were right, we had given names to the fish that rested on them. We went there in groups and we fished socially, sometimes flipping a coin to see who would go through the pool first.

Back then, it seemed as if there was always a group of youth hanging out at my parents' farmhouse. Our place was like an inclusive, homestyle angling club, one with a long arm that reached out to new members, especially those from out of province and the USA. This may have been inspired by my mother's fine cooking, or the family's traditional interest in fly-fishing, I don't know. Certainly, we all ate well. And we fished well. In fact we lived in the art of fly-casting day and night like a group of academics might consume themselves with a certain thesis. It seemed as though we were never discussing anything but food and drink, boats and waders, rods and reels, lines and fly hooks, as if there were no other world outside these things, none that mattered to us in the least, and that anarchy was the fashionable vice. We ignored the outside world and its problems with a sense of arrogance. So obsessed were we with the river and fly-fishing, that not even the agonies of far-off wars or famines or the excitement of the new space-age travel got through to us for very long: this was the same obsessive spirit that later guided us through our professional careers.

After an evening's angling at Rum Rock, when the shadows of nightfall had overtaken us and another darkness was settling in, we headed back home. We poled our canoes against the stronger currents, where we knew the water was deeper, until we were able to make our way, sometimes in the moonlight, up the hill on the old truck-wagon road to my parents' farmhouse. There, light beamed from the kitchen windows and the open door of the adjacent woodshed to illuminate the back part of the dooryard. We hung our rods and waders on a rack in the veranda, pattered into the living room where we drank a toast to the day's experiences, "To the scales and the tails of our uncaptured bounty," and then stood around the piano while my brother Gary played and we sang folk and traditional songs into the night, until the last one standing had wandered off to bed. It was a ritual repeated the next day, and the next—neither planned in advance nor mentioned afterwards—but assumed by everyone who was staying on the property.

Americans out of university for the summer, young men like David Egan and Louie Eagle, came from Connecticut to stay, sometimes with their girlfriends, for weeks at a time, welcomed as part of the family. For them everything here was a learning experience, a kind of real-life summer camp without hard rules or a curfew but with a very real river where the wild salmon were plenty. They also came "home" for their honeymoons, bunked in one of our cabins, and in Miramichi fashion, were chivareed with the beating of tin pots and the firing of shotguns. This was a celebration that our circle of friends imposed on one another on our wedding nights, getting the bride and groom out of bed, to join the party, have another drink—and then again for Christmas and New Year's.

My mother and father enjoyed having so many young people around; they loved the music and the laughter that came from that large old front parlour that my mother kept cool during the day by closing the curtains and draping an awning of damp towels over the wood-scrolled screen door. We all shared the same imaginings, the same rural gothic. There were Marilyn Monroe sightings to report (it was said that Marilyn—dead by then—had fished here in the fifties with her husband Joe DiMaggio) and kangaroo sightings (one of these animals had escaped from a circus in the forties and was never recaptured), things that had been part of Miramichi folklore for decades. Indeed, the place had become an escape where all concerned could breathe in a fresh scent of freedom, stretch the imagination as far as possible. And we soaked it up.

We practised river etiquette and conservation, too. We were adamant about these beliefs, especially when it came to the environment and its species. By the early seventies, we had already started to release our big salmon. David Egan went back to New Haven and founded the Connecticut River Salmon Association (CRSA), which is still going strong; those of us who wrote preached conservation in our articles and books.

For me, those were unforgettable years, a time when my family and our angling friends let our vanities drift away like foam on the water. We all marched to the same tune, the belief that it was the person you lived and angled with and not his social status, politics, or money that mattered. It was a place where reality ended and illusion began. The old river served as the equalizer in that regard.

Each of us practised our own spiritual beliefs, but the joy of a clear conscience reigned supreme for us all. It was a time to be enjoyed to the fullest, without feeling the shame of being looked upon as free-spirited layabouts; we were just loving people. Loves like those will never come our way again. And even now, when I go to Rum Rock, I can feel this. While the place has taken on a new spirit, my musings are steeped into the water and the landscape: that old place of freedom.

Photographs of that era show the group of us standing together against some cabin or shed, with our fishing tackle in hand. We were armed with the big five-ounce, fibreglass rods and the iron-hooped landing nets that today are seen only in museums—glass rods clamped in iron hands, spruce poles bending in the rushing waters of spring. I see my brothers, sister, and I, along with our spouses or would-be spouses, young women with their long hair, bare feet, peasant skirts, and expressing their budding feminism, smoking a Wrangler cigar or holding a drink of rum in a brown paper bag. Like the picturesque fashions and free-thinking world of the sixties and early seventies, we had let the river take us over, impose its addictions and obsessions on us.

In fact we were so intoxicated by the river that we could taste it in our pre-dinner soups, as well as the after-dinner liquors. We could smell it in the breezes of passing cars and motorboats, in the suntan lotion and insect sprays that we rubbed onto our skin. We could hear it in the sounds of toads that sang on the water, the harmony of shorebirds, the eagle and the nighthawk's lonely cry, and especially in the songs of Joni Mitchell and John Denver: "River" and "Thank God I'm A Country Boy."

My ex-wife, Janet Manderville, came with me to Rum Rock. She had also perfected the long cast, the angle of the swing and the retrieve action required. She hooked and released salmon, too. We had fished there many times in the late sixties and early seventies and we always used the single, barbless hooks and we never killed a fish, by accident or on purpose. And I can still remember the cool morning breezes, the brilliant sky where little white clouds made dancing reflections on the water as the sun strengthened to penetrate our cotton shirts—unforgettable summer days.

Once in an early July thunderstorm—which, according to Papa, kills the horseflies, causes snakes to shed their skin, and shatters the fragile eggs under nesting hens—we huddled in the shore grass under the overturned canoe. We had gone there in field clothing, without rain gear of any kind. Talking in monotones against the echo of the canoe's hollowness and the spill of rain, we watched as the big silver drops hit the water's surface like bird shot to form bubbles that dissolved and drifted away in widening rings and clouded the water near the shore. After the shower, we continued casting through the cooler, rain-washed afternoon, the fish more active on the rise.

Another time, because there was no lightning, we fished right through the shower, drawing our canvas hoods up tightly around our faces like wetsuits, the raincoat tails covering the tops of our wading boots to keep us dry.

"I feel like a duck out here," Janet said, her translucent blue eyes flashing under the hood. "But I want to stay!"

I never took anyone to Rum Rock who didn't have the same romantic feelings about the place as I did. It was an atmosphere unlike any I have experienced anywhere else in the world.

My friends and I fished at the Rum Rock, took turns in a rotation of twos, as was the established ritual, and found relief from the penetrating sunshine under the visor of a pine tree branch. That blinding old sun drove the frogs and turtles under water, faded our life jackets, blistered the paint on our log cabins, and has long since turned our skin into the tongues of leather moccasins, our hair into dusters of cotton candy.

As the years passed, my brothers, sister, and I, and sometimes a friend from away, still went there as before, when the breath of autumn drifted in. Once in a while my father, who loved the river with great passion, came with us, though more and more seldom. The pool was still fishing well, although it was pretty much vacated by then. And a lot of the magic had gone from the scene, as many from our age had grown and moved on to the outside world, to bigger and more exciting things. Some had given up fly-fishing completely. Our reasons for going there were different than before. And so the atmosphere was different.

Later in the fall, as the upriver winds blew across our stubble fields and the shore grass tossed in waves of thatch, I went there with Daddy for the last few times. He was well into his senior years by then, tiring and frail. It was not easy for him to throw a casting line into those against-the-flow autumnal gales. And the wild Canada geese that were heading south glided in and skated to a stop, where they tossed about on the waves like honking decoys. We huddled in our wool sweaters and gloves, built bonfires on the shore, smoked cigars, drank a toddy, and turned our backs to urinate downwind, as in the old days. We closed down the season with a toast to summers past—"one for the ages"—and to our old friends who had gone back to Upper Canada, the United States, even to Europe, and had taken up the more worldly causes, so long, long ago. Autumn, that golden season of the years, that age when, if we listen carefully, we can hear the good years whispering behind our backs. For it is in those moments one remembers one's youth as being somewhere between perfection and divinity. And I search a deserted countryside for a new Eden with a sad realization that it "just ain't gonna happen." Because Rum Rock was a youthful state of mind more than it was a geographic location.

By this time, too, the new romances and distractions in my life are mostly hypothetical. Or in my dreams. The electronic world is forbidden and unfriendly. Still, I savour the hours and I never stop reading and writing in the hopes that my mind will stay active, just a while longer. But I know there is no real formula to prevent the inevitable.

Sometimes, if the spirit is not being poached by loud people who are not river lovers, I go to Rum Rock with a literary friend. We shoot holes into the breeze as we discuss the challenges of writing, the business of publishing, and the politics of getting good reviews in this day and age. Novelist David Adams Richards accompanies me to the Rock at least three times each summer, as does writer Tony Tremblay. Together we fish as we solve the world's social and literary problems.

Sometimes, too, my friend Paola Thurrott and I paddle there in my father's old Chestnut canoe. Together we stand in the boat, and consumed in animated conversation, we take turns throwing a line, starting with just the leader, as I had learned to do so long ago, inching our way out as far as we can reach, while watching the water for a fish to rise. I am trying to teach this young woman how to fly cast.

"They are still here," I tell her. "There is always a salmon lying just beyond that little dimple at centre stream."

And as we angle, for a moment, I can sense those carefree days from the sixties and early seventies, right there in the water and the penetrating sunshine, like friends who live on in the silences, who emerge from the shadows but then disappear just as quickly. And for an instant, I find myself trying to grasp and hold onto them, before they are replaced by another moment, another decade. It's all so fleeting.

River Camp

When I was a small boy, long before I had started school and before my parents actually allowed me to go to the river, I stole away to spend my afternoons sitting behind a pine tree, watching the sport anglers at their game. Well hidden from their view, I was so near these people I could smell their sweet-scented tobacco smoke, feel the excitement in their voices, hear their hearty chuckles as I stood witness to the many salmon they hooked and brought to the boat. I kept a count of the fish each one caught, the time of day it happened, and who from the community was guiding them. It was just a childish game I played while waiting for the day when I could afford a rod and reel and would be allowed go to the river to angle as the adults were doing.

Through April and most of May, in front of our place, the river was deep, slow moving. Despite the wind, which dried the laundry my mother hung on her clothesline "right well," and the choppy water, which was like the seas where Jesus walked in the Sunday school pamphlets, there was always someone with a fish on the line. The split bamboo rods bowed, and their steel ferrules glittered in the sunlight. And I can still see the river guides—my father and uncles among them—their coat collars turned up, dip-nets in hand, as they stood in the boat and stared into the dark moving waters, while they waited for the fish to be brought to the surface. Ninety-nine percent of those spring salmon were scooped and released back into the water, even then.

They fished that way until five in the afternoon, when the guides pulled their anchors, started their Johnson Seahorse outboard motors, and headed upriver to the outfitter's camp. Their boats threw a muddied swell upon our sodden shore and—because they had gone upstream—left the water's surface choppy long after the sound of their motors were out of earshot. Sometimes I stayed at the river until a parent came, scolding, to drag me home.

It seems when you grow up on a river it is a part of you forever. As an adult you can live anywhere in the world, the most exotic places imaginable, but you are never completely content unless you are on or near a river, preferably the home stream. You may become financially successful, famous, even loved, but you never feel that everything is completely right with the world until you are back on the water that has been flowing through your veins, since even before you were born. For we remain a part of the landscape and riverscape in which we were conceived and raised, just as our parents and grandparents had been. I believe that river people are like salmon, homing cranes, or robins in that regard; and so we return to build camps or cottages where we spend our hard-earned holiday time and dollars in the hopes of reclaiming a piece of the old river spirit we had so many years before.

Having moved away from the river as a teenager to live in a big city through most of the sixties, pining for that river life was a dilemma I had to deal with. I was doing well financially and had made a new home and friends in Ontario. But I secretly missed the old stream and the outdoor life I had left behind. While I knew the farm community as I remembered it, was long gone, and the ways of my boyhood had become insignificant, I still wanted to build a cabin on the home property and near the river. And I now believe this was in the planning stages, though perhaps subconsciously, even as I was leaving home, indeed, ever since those pre-school days of river watching.

Each summer when I came home on vacation, I went to the woods with my father, where we cut a few logs and hauled them to the campsite with his old horse Jenny, an animal that had brought Santa Claus to our house many times. I also hauled rocks in the trunk of my car for the foundation and fireplace. I had planned then on building in the early seventies, when I had saved enough money, but I knew it would be a life-long project.

I moved from Ontario in the spring of sixty-nine, purchased a farmhouse in the estuary, and went into the furniture business. Having lived in the city for years (except for long summer vacations), I could not get enough of the country life. My farmhouse—which years before had housed a blacksmith—was ghostly and cold, but it had a parlour fireplace, some nice oak and maple trees on the property, and Virginia creeper vines that smothered the open veranda, indeed a great spirit. I lived there with my small family and eventually restored the house to its former resplendence, complete with wood screen doors and shutters, canvas awnings, and clay chimney pots. During this time, to experience the river life more closely, my wife and I and the children sometimes camped out in a floorless tent or our Chevy station wagon, fought mosquitoes and bad weather, and drank brook water while we cooked on open campfires. It was five years before I was in a position to start the cabin's construction.

In the fall of seventy-four, my father and I laid foundation stones on land he had deeded to me, under the same old tree where, as a boy, I had sat to watch the river. On Thanksgiving Monday, we started putting up the walls, one log at a time. It was a slow and back-breaking process—three or four logs on each wall, every day—because those timbers had to be notched at the corners and carefully dove-tailed into place. Having spent his lifetime in the woods and in building log camps for the lumber trade, my father knew what to do: he was an excellent axeman. He meticulously made the notches and together with a block and line we hoisted the pine and spruce logs up a ramp and placed them carefully on the growing cribwork, until we had the walls in place and the second-hand doors and windows firmly installed. Then we stood on pole beams and fitted hand-hewn rafters together, boarded in and shingled the roof.

The weather stayed fine and we had the cabin up and the cracks caulked with ropes of oakum by the end of November.

Before winter set in, we built a veranda facing the river. It was cold out there so close to the water at that time of year—there were snowflakes in the air and chunks of ice adrift—especially after the sun had dropped down into the woods. We put the last few shingles on the veranda roof in the sub-zero short twilight.

In early December we set up a cast-iron stove and smoke pipes, and after building a big fire of spruce and pine blocks, which made the stove puff and pant and the pipes creak and rattle, we installed the partitions and interior doors. While there was still much to do, by the spring of seventy-five—after running a water pipe from the swamp well—my family was able to go there and spend the night. It was like getting a fix for an old, hard-fought addiction.

This was an exciting time for my then-wife Janet Manderville (who had also been born on this river and was a river person before I met her in Ontario), for my sons, Jeff, Jason, and Steven, and for me. While the boys played their new or perhaps not-so-new river games, Janet made tablecloths and quilts and stocked the kitchen with dishes she had picked up at yard sales. We acquired new and used furniture and added screens to the windows and doors.

By the long weekend in May, when we had our official opening, the cabin was cozy and warm and there were plenty of folding chairs for everyone we had invited to help us christen our new place, Camp Oriole—named for a fly hook I had used with great success as a boy.

In the early evening of May 23, cars and pickup trucks started to arrive. And there was the usual honking of horns, the blatting of faulty mufflers, the revving-up of gas-fumed engines, until our yard and adjacent fields were filled with vehicles of all shapes and sizes. And there was a great deal of shouting and whooping. People milled about, smoked tobacco, and drank whiskey from bottles in brown paper bags. There was the tuning of musical instruments, the twang of broken strings, and the impulsive, robust laughter. It seemed everyone had brought a bottle of spirits, plus fiddles, banjos, guitars, and mouth organs. There were no electronic sounds, as we were still in the process of getting the hydro power installed. Tin lanterns and candles were lit as we synchronized the instruments to a standard pitch. And we sang the folk songs of Bob Dylan, James Taylor, Gordon Lightfoot, Joan Baez, and Joni Mitchell, along with a hundred other songs and poems we had written ourselves. I played my old fiddle, as I had done at the Blackville dance halls as a boy, and the women scuffed around in a square-dance fashion.

The crowd grew in numbers and spirit, and eventually spilled out onto the veranda and hillside, until my father's field was one big musical celebration. It seemed as if everyone who lived on the river came to celebrate our camp. It was like the folk festivals (Woodstock and others), which were so common in that day. As the night went on, we celebrated not only our camp but also a dozen other events: my brother Herbie's wedding, my sister's December birthday, the christening of Steven, my youngest son, my father and mother's anniversary, and so on. The party grew louder and sometime in the night our neighbours, who were a half-kilometre away, complained. The Mounties came and told us to "keep it down." And I can remember thinking at first, what do people have against the freedom of expression? And then I realized, they are right of course, we have to keep it down, respect the silences of the night, our neighbour's right to hear the wildlife at their song.

The party lasted until the break of day, when everyone started to drift homeward. And I watched the sun rise over the teeth of my mother's picket fence, which, from that distance and that angle, looked like a row of little white crosses at the graveyard in Flanders. Janet and I were left trying to figure out where the clean-up should commence.

In the ten years that followed, my family and I spent all our summers at Camp Oriole. We moved there when school ended in June and stayed until Labour Day. I was still in the furniture business and was commuting to Newcastle, a half-hour's drive each way. My sons grew up on the river as I did. They canoed, swam, built dykes, panned for baby eels, and fly-fished. My son Jason kept a vegetable garden. The boys hooked, landed, and released their first Atlantic salmon when each one was seven years old. Looking back, I believe it was the best early life they could have had because they learned so much first-hand about the river and the woods and how to respect all forms of wildlife. When they became adults, they built camps on the home stream. For sure, the river camp had long since become a family tradition.

Back then, during my summer holidays, we fished trout on weekend excursions to Morse Brook when the days were hot and sultry, and we brought home fish for the breakfast frying pan. At night, under the board roof of our cabin (which was poorly ventilated and without air conditioning), we sat up late and listened to music because it was almost impossible to get a full night's sleep, especially if there was no cooling river breeze to whisper through that front screen door. Of course, we didn't need much sleep at that time in our lives and wanted to make the most of our days and nights on the river. And there was always someone dropping by at some late hour who wanted to party with us. We set up oscillating fans on tables to help circulate the air and propped open the windows, but the place stayed warm long into the morning hours. The children went to sleep in a screened-in gazebo I had built on the sundeck. And through the long nights, as June bugs butted against the screens, the sounds of toads singing and frogs croaking in the big cedar swamp back of the camp coloured our dreams, constant reminders that we were at the river, which was a comfort to us all. Up early—for we were all young and filled with energy—we packed a lunch and canoed the wild rivers and hiked to the turbulent trout streams for our breakfast dish. We barbecued and had fondue parties while Bob Dylan sang "Don't Think Twice, It's All Right."

I remember sitting on a stool by a card table in that little screen-house and writing articles for the wildlife magazines I contributed to in those days. This was before the age of computers and I was using an old iron typewriter with letters that would not punch out clearly and a cylinder that jammed the paper, which frustrated me. I can still hear the "snap, snap,

snap" of the keys on that old Remington because they had to be driven down hard—with one finger—to make even the most subtle impressions. I still type that way.

Sometimes, in the heat of the afternoon, I took a break from my work and went to the river where the children were fishing or perhaps building a raft of cedar poles for one of their moonlight excursions. And I fished with them or worked with them while doing some necessary cooling down and getting a bit of "live" research and inspiration for my story. This was where the mysterious, log-size sturgeon had lived in my great-grandfather's time. This was where the legendary river drives and the salmon netting parties had taken place when Papa was a young man. This was where, in my father's day, the spring motorboats jostled for position to troll the salmon lies, and where the ghost of a man, who drowned doing this, haunted the family because he had stayed in our cabin and used our canoe. This was where, as a boy, I built a skating rink for our evening bonfires, the great games of hockey. And the long-abandoned spooky farmhouse where I attended my first wake could be seen on the opposite hillside. In the moonlight, its windows were blank, the coffin still in the parlour.

In the autumn, my sons and I dressed in orange and with Shane, our old Irish setter, running beside us, we went to the alder swamps to look for partridge or woodcock. We celebrated Thanksgiving Sunday with the larger family and a roasted turkey. And to close the place, we always had a big potluck meal and a hoedown when the season was over.

Sometimes in winter we went back to Camp Oriole, when

there was snow on the trees and the river had frozen over. We built up the fires—it took a full day to get the dampness out of the bedclothes and the sofa chairs—and we went out to skate on the river ice; the only music came from the chickadees. In the evening we sat by the open fire to enjoy a hot drink and a good meal, while hailstones tapped on the windows.

The great days that one can remember from a lifetime—the youthful experiences that stand in the mind like shade trees in a pasture—can be counted on the fingers of one hand. They appear and disappear ever so quickly and are replaced perhaps by memories that have been inspired from a different day, even longer ago.

But here, at the camp, things are deep flowing, deeper rooted. With a fire crackling in the big stone fireplace, a glass of good wine in hand, and some jazz on the CD player, I can sit in front of the picture window, unnoticed, and watch those April fishers at their game. Yes, they are still here. And even though I am now old and looking for God, because I am hard of hearing in my right ear and hard of sight in my left eye, this is like a happy return to childhood.

I marvel at how the seasons of the year and the seasons of life silently repeat themselves. I'm waiting for my grandsons Samuel and Joshua, who will soon be arriving from the city with their parents. Tomorrow we are going to build a raft.

River Spirits

After a windy April morning on the river we were chilled to the bone. Some of us gathered in the guide's camp to warm ourselves. As we stood in a circle and held our reddened hands to the fire, someone in the group suggested we put fifty cents each into a collection to buy a bottle of spirits from the camp's owner. All agreed. One of my fellow workers, a man from upriver, whom I did not know well, was out of cash, so I tossed his share into the hat. We got a bottle of white rum, which was passed around only once before it was empty. This little treat heated our insides and lifted our spirits, infusing us with a shot of self-confidence as we set in at the dining-room table for the noonday meal.

Three months later, I was coming out of the woods when I saw a dump truck stop in front of my home and then pull away. When I reached the house, I was told that the driver had stopped to repay the money he'd borrowed from me. I had forgotten all about it. Still, this was a nice surprise, because in 1960 fifty cents would buy a pack of cigarettes, an order of fish and chips, or get me into a show at the old movie house in

Blackville. It would take two or three hours to earn that kind of money in the woods or on the river.

But what was more important was that I had discovered how thoughtful and honest my neighbour was. That little recollection has stayed with me through the years. It was the beginning of a river relationship with no ending.

A lifetime later, this same friend and I talked about taking a canoe trip down the Cains River some melancholy day when summer was coming to an end. And what a perfect way it would have been to recapture the spirit of our youth, to drift together on that stream, where he had been born and raised, and where my great-grandmother Maggie Porter's home had been, and whose waters flowed through our veins. However, we were not so foolish as to be cheated by the illusions of nostalgia, which can separate the heart's yearning from reality, a kind of decay brought on by the years. No, we just wanted to go there, see once more its pine-treed hillsides, taste its barren-fed waters, smell its shore flowers, hear its freshet sounds, which carry in them such a big part of our life's genealogy. And these things, we felt, would enhance the old family spirits we were seeking, each of us in our own secret way.

Many times, by chance, we met in Blackville's Value Village and discussed our river run, although it appeared less likely to happen as time went by. He was much older than I and his health had started to fail him. And while these discussions went on, it was obvious to me that Cains River had become a place where longing took us, for as we talked about the trip, each of us was sharing our most poignant and memorable moments.

He is gone now, may he rest in peace, but I suspect his spirit is on that river. As mine is, through that bond of ancestry, the recollection of his friendship and our mutual desire to go back there, and the inspiration to write this essay. Someday, perhaps in another life, my friend and I will do that canoe run. Spiritually, I think we have done it already.

The river spirit is hard to explain to a non-river person. To understand it fully, you'd have to have grown up in the river environment, to have experienced first-hand its soul, its moods, its superstitions, its people, and the sense of freedom and love the river brought them. It's a thing impossible to articulate to someone from outside the river community—and sometimes even to other, less sensitive, less observant river people who do not feel the stream literally—how the spirit of the moving water and the landscape, the way these things have been embedded in our psyche through the years, inspire human affection and bonding. For we are drawn together, not only through our mutual love for the life, the river itself, but even the groves, hills, and meadows that surround the water come into play. They are like props or landmarks that contribute to the spirit of the stream that flows among them. Each of these things combines to create a different state of mind for each of us—our love for the place where the old home used to stand, the fields of wildflowers now overgrown with shrubbery and trees, the invisible clapboard school from where the river could be seen as we recited our allegiance to the flag, and which brings back the memories of so many loved ones who have long since departed this life. For we, the river people, are in a sense like an unstructured cult held together in a pleasurable environment by a flow that runs through the land, the geologic umbilical that connects us, at least in spirit.

These feelings are brought about by our love for the river and the experiences we've had on or near the water, or even those we wish to have had—like that canoe trip with my friend that never happened. These encounters are unconsciously shared, whether we are together or apart and can be set spinning by an image as subtle as a dragonfly wing, the sound of an osprey's cry, or the scent of a shore's dogwood blossom. They are like the pockets of happiness you might experience when hiking in an old familiar wood, where you have shared unforgettable outings with a parent, a sibling, or a lover. Through the magic of metaphor, we are united.

We return to such mood-setting places, when the conditions are the same as how we remember them, to relive the memories these surroundings have inspired in us. They are brought back to life not only through visual landmarks, which are linked to some feeling, but also in the acoustics of the setting, the hollowness of the air, the taste of a berry, the scents of the earth, or even the sounds of the wind whispering in the trees. For country people are very much in tune with the landscape and riverscape we inhabit. In the same way that the inland soul is less visionary when it comes to the river life, yet is so connected to non-river experiences so remote to river people. Like the street savvy and the mutual bonding of habit that exists among long-time city people. It's a question of familiarity and what effect these places have on the soul through a lifetime.

These images and the spirits they bring forth are deeper

than science and they speak a higher language. They are the God-like soul movements that arise from the most heartfelt recollections and live inside me somewhere between life itself and books. Any single one of these symbols can trigger an experience from years ago, and suddenly I am with an old friend (or enemy) and in that place and time, reliving precious, or perhaps not so precious, memories. And this experience endures long after that person is dead, as in the cases of my mother and father or other loved ones. This is especially the case with good memories, since our souls have a healing power that keeps us from going back to trauma.

When we are on the river or in that river spirit, time does not exist. It's as if we are in a dream world from which we are eventually awakened, not because time has run out but we have exhausted all our emotions. This state of mind is not usually shared outside the river community; rather, it's an affection between the river and its prospective lovers. There are moods of joy or self-assurance perhaps invigorated by the sun and the sparkling waters of spring, to those of complacency felt on hazy summer days, to the melancholy thoughts of apathy (and sometimes separation) stirred by an autumnal turbulence, to the uneasiness and worry inspired by the haunting ice surface of a winter's day where the only river sounds are the squawks of ravens—the bird of ill omen that follows the scent of death. For sure, each season has its own moods that bring with them their own innocence and healing state of mind.

These "spirit" images (on the earth and the water), once experienced, remain in the back of our minds forever and some have even been passed down, perhaps unconsciously, from previous generations. Through the years, we have heard our elders tell and retell something that has happened to them on that very spot and on the kind of day and time of year in question, which no doubt has served to inspire its recounting. So that we remember it, again, on one such day years later. Sometimes I think our influences come from the dead, more than the living, especially for those of us of a mature age, who have heard these things many times and who are more sensitive to the elements and their messages. Like a former love who can read from our sighs that we are troubled, that we have been dwelling, perhaps too long, on what might have been and blaming everyone but ourselves for who we have become since their loss.

In some ways, these spirit symbols are like those undulations felt in the ambience that surrounds a vacated beach in the Caribbean before a winter's holiday, mood-setting images so often used by travel agencies to sell places in the mind more than the geographical destination. Or perhaps they are carried in your first encounter on an Alpine range, the spirit of the mountains, which can be spooky, or in a First Nations burial ground in the North, or in an expanse of windblown, open prairie in the old Canadian West. Or maybe it's the feelings you experience when you stop to observe a forlorn sunset or the low clouds on a dark windy day before a winter blizzard—storm fear. There is a certain energy in each of these, a kind of soul movement.

This is similar to the awareness of mood found in a magnificent piece of artwork, a grand old tree, a weather-beaten and sunken barn standing in an overgrown field, or the aura that accompanies a certain piece of classical music. Other such soul nourishments, for me, may be brought to the surface by a dreary train whistle or a distant church bell on a crisp, clear Sunday morning. These things, like river images, take me to special places in the mind. And there is a heartfelt, godly atmosphere that can be found in such places as old churches because the sensitive architect had designed the place to release these feeling in those of us who go there to pray or meditate, or in a cool, tree-shaded manor house, set well back from a city street, a place not designed to create a mood, rather it grew there through time and from an old family's spirit that just would not die.

When I go to such places alone, I can feel the presence and the love of all of those with whom I have shared that environment, or even those I wanted to share it with through the years. And these feelings are experienced at different times by those who have enjoyed these good memories with me. Though separated now, we remain joined together in spirit. It's a kind of magical realism, where robins yodel, jays cry, horses chuckle, waters babble, and trees whisper, one that can be set spinning by a simple sound bite. It is mind power that is far beyond any form of technology and so is not communicable. And this is something that the electronic age cannot compete with because such moods cannot be transmitted or observed on a computer screen.

This spirit is one I feel briefly when I meet a fellow river person on my city street and because of our mutual love for similar things, our shared sensitivities, there is a platonic embrace, physically and, yes, spiritually. We are in a relationship. We rehash a few old excitements, incomprehensible to non-river people, and make a brief plan to experience yet another, which may or may not come about. It doesn't matter. We have the same dreams and want to make them happen. Now, as we mature, we love these things more than ever, and more openly and honestly. We have nothing left to prove beyond the joys of the river and its surroundings, no new influences to follow, and we know that our eternal rest is growing near. It's like planting our feet, and our feelings, in places where they were always meant to be. And we have triumphed in this at last like a child who keeps on attempting to turn a handspring or a cartwheel, until she succeeds and moves on to other things. She will return to the cartwheel and its thrills, at least in her dreams, forever after.

When I first came home from Ontario after being away from the river for a few years, I was driving along the banks of the Little Southwest Miramichi. At a place called Red Stone, the scenery was so spectacular that I stopped the car, got out, and stood awhile to soak up the river's spirit. I was standing there in meditation, watching the water, when a non-river passerby stopped and asked if I was okay. Not wanting to tell him that I was there to observe what spirit the place had to offer, I said that I had heard a noise in my motor.

"Start 'er up," he said as he put his ear to the engine. "Yes, I can hear it, too," he said. "It's your camshaft."

There may be dozens of pedestrians walking past me on the sidewalk, people with whom I have shared many commercial, and perhaps even artistic, experiences along the way. They pass me with a "hello" and a tip of the hat. These are not the same as the connections made with fellow river souls, when for a brief moment, our two spirits mingle and become as one on a given stretch of water. (It's like strangers who fall in together at a party and play music by ear, and whose souls share the common delight. Or how individual works of art from a certain school or movement resemble one another.) And the longer we chat about the influences that our days on the water have excited in us—either together or apart—the more our family characteristics unite. I don't know of any other object in nature that enkindles a better bonding, except perhaps the mountains for their people. It is hard to stay in the city and on the job after an encounter like that, hard to concentrate on anything unrelated to the river.

These same feelings may be shared, I suppose, when two writers or actors or dog lovers get together, or when two old loves reunite and for a brief moment the fire burns anew. It's a bonding that pulls people by the heartstrings, the connection of having shared the passion for a given time and place in the mind. It's a spirit that is as fleeting and as abstract as a snowflake that melts before it reaches the ground. Yet it is very real for those of us who have experienced the snowflake's descent. It's like grasping at the shadows of blackbirds that flit about the gravestones in our family burial grounds. Indeed, there is no language to convey these heart-shared feelings to people who are wrong to the sounds and scenes, so can never hear or see them.

And there are the shared river myths, the dreams, the superstitions, the ghosts, and the religions. These can be experienced from something as subtle as the moon's tint at a certain time of evening, the squawk of a bird on a certain kind of day, the rustling of a tree combined with a certain fragrance, the scent of the water before a storm, or the sentimental red and purple of post-sunset skies. Just a few foretelling symbols to be observed, enjoyed, or heeded to.

For decades I have been trying to create a distinct spirit in my river cabin. There are few sounds in that place (except in my memory), only the smells of tar and boat oakum, and the view of log walls, the lingering taste of home-cooked meals, which carry in them the days when my father and I built the place, when my boys were small, my family and river friends were together, and times were happier. And I know, too, that these feelings cannot be fully shared, except through happenstance. So I am catering to a small circle; the ones who were there, or wished to have been there, in the seventies. In a sense, I am catering to myself.

It is thirty-seven years since the cabin was constructed, so I want it to look and feel very much a part of that place and time. Yet, in some ways I want it to appear like the kind of setting that is loaded with history and the river's carefree culture, so enjoyed by us during those wonderful years, and which, I hope, the passing of time will enhance. (Similar to the New England country inns from the nineteenth century, where writers like Longfellow and Hawthorne gathered before the fire to swap yarns, settings which are still alive with these men's spirits and so are now considered national treasures.)

My place will never be a treasure to anyone but me, and I hope, the people I have shared it with, or may still share it with. I have no illusions of grandeur.

I have painted the logs dark brown, installed a stone (now ivy-clad) fireplace, and above the mantel I have hung a mounted salmon that my grandfather caught one hundred years ago. I am in search of an ancient roll-top desk and an out-of-date globe, a glass-fronted bookcase, and some classic Chippendale wing-back chairs, which I will place before the fire to be enjoyed on rainy autumn nights after a day on the water. I am also in search of two nineteenth-century candy-stripe awnings to droop over the shuttered windows to help keep the place cool on summer days. A bouquet of wildflowers stands on the dining-room table. And in the library, some old readers from my elementary school days, a time in my life when those great stories and poems were implanted into my consciousness, the spirit of which—by means of the old home and river setting in which they were studied—has been kept alive to this day.

This is not the way my place looked in the seventies, rather it is how I felt the cabin should look, and so it is the dream place I carried inside me rather than the actual cabin itself. This while I struggled to understand the poetry of Leonard Cohen and Rod McKuen, and my portable hi-fi monopolized the songs of Bob Dylan and Gordon Lightfoot, all symbols of the era. I cannot say exactly what I am trying to design in the way of a cultural décor, rather it's more a river spirit and my family's place therein. There has been no great atmosphere captured or preserved until this point.

Such a spirit is almost impossible to create, like a short story before it has been written in that it is hard to grasp the tale's source, still an undeveloped inspiration in the writer's mind. And such spirit probably cannot be bought with dollars from any marketplace or commercial designer. But when it comes to my cabin, I do know where its roots stem from. If it lacks taste, it does not lack originality. I will be content when I have finished it to my own best standards. I only hope that the ambience will follow, for me and for others who come after me. But I doubt if anyone else in the family cares a damn about such abstract things, the pulse of an old community that is already long gone and which no one but me is trying to recapture.

And there is the view from my picture window. Never the same any two days, or two hours in a row, nor are the feelings that this scene inspires, with its moving waters, changing shorelines, the sun's reflections, and wind movements, moods only for those of us who have witnessed them before and return to in some measure.

From life in general, I have also found that, like a river, there is a certain spirit that surrounds a celebrity. And I believe these vibes come from the idea that these people are loved and their causes and their art are shared by so many like-minded people. It comes from originality, hard work, and the soul of the creator. I have felt this when I was in the presence of Leonard Cohen, Bob Dylan, Willie Nelson, and Paul Simon and Art Garfunkel. There is a kind of magic that surrounds these bigger-than-life people, an atmosphere that is part artistic, part humanitarian, and one that touches the heartstrings of a broad-reaching family every time their music is heard. This can also be said of the more refined listener who enjoys classical music. The composers have said something in the melodies that we were waiting to hear but didn't have the talent to create. We know these people attained their greatness because of hard work, talent, and imagination, qualities many of us share but to lesser degrees. And so we are their fans. They are our inspiration.

While I may no longer feel that I have the personal attractions to please, or the strength to love anyone as I once did, neither can I fall into step with the youth of today (whose music and poetry are hard for me to comprehend and which for me carry absolutely no magic), I believe the river has become a place that will entice new people into my life. Maybe that river spirit will bring them back to me, physically. For the river has also become an equalizer in that it helps me nurture friendships that have gone sour and to relive, even glorify, the good ones that I hold onto like old loves.

While at my age the desires of the flesh are deadening, those of the mind are strengthening, so that I could love, in the true sense of the word, more than ever. And understand more easily the things I struggled with so long ago. It has that kind of healing power, the river has.

Even people who are long dead, like my father and grandfather, are brought back to me when I go to these special places in the mind. And their causes and actions that I rebelled against are now more tolerable, if not completely understood. It says in the Bible that we never outlive our parents. This could also be said of people with whom we've had great experiences. Or old loves. Or even home. In this sense, originality and familiarity are more precious than a broad-reaching knowledge, more lasting than a moss-covered rhyme on a marble gravestone, and are for me the greater homage. In truth, when it comes to a lasting affection, the moment retrieved is more important than the chiselled word.

In a reoccurring dream, I am walking, barefoot, through a field of wildflowers on a warm and tranquil Sunday morning, when the sky is clear and a light breeze makes the daisies, the buttercups, and the devil's paintbrushes stroke me with their moist and woolly stems. The purple-blossomed timothy and the seedy fine-top tickle my knees while the chickweed crowds between my toes to break my stride. And I abruptly slow, like a giant who has been dragged down by his shackles. There is grasshopper spit in the undergrowth where the insect scampers on legs bent like the long arms of post-hole diggers and whose transparent wings are those of a glass drop-leaf table. It makes buzzing sounds like when our lights are on and a June bug hits our window screens. And butterflies come and go on silent wings, up and down, up and down, into my face and away, to teeter on a ripened stem and fight the morning breeze, which makes the dried grass rattle like the dead cornstalks of autumn. The flutter of small birds that fly out of the grass is so delicate it is to be pursued only by the minds of curious children. For a brief moment I am young again and looking for a hidden nest, the pearly eggs of blue speckled with white.

I can smell the river, which is blinking beyond a hedge of trees, hear its chuckles and babbles, feel its welcoming coolness. And suddenly an old piece of music, one I've heard in schools and churches comes back to me. This brings a loved one from my adolescence, so long ago, to walk beside me in this field of wildflowers and across the wire bridge to her home. Though long dead, she is as real and as beautiful as the day that I had been wounded by her passions. And suddenly I'm thinking that this just might be the most beautiful place on the earth in which to live. Her presence—so young and innocent—which is still here, has made it so. For a brief moment the teachings from school and church come to mind and I feel that I will be forever young, perhaps in another life, with the ones who remember me. You see, love works two ways.

I pray the people who once lived in that farmhouse that stood upon the hill and who come back to me on lonely winter nights, will not return with a scythe and rake to mow this field of wildflowers, this interval of dreams, and stack it into ricks of thatch, cart it away to threshing barns to be beaten and eaten by animals on snowy January evenings. And leave a notation of mere stubble to bruise feet, scatter nests, and frighten field mice, while slaying the stems from which the butterfly could roost, yielding to the chuckle beyond the hedge, the laughter and love beyond the bridge, while silencing the love music of birds, and turning the summer into autumn with the simple strokes of a scythe. According to our mothers and fathers, once the hay is cut the summer is gone, and our thoughts must change to school days and golden songs and wood poems and blowing leaves and moonlit nights and fires that warm us against the burn of frost, which turns the after-grass into a cowhide, with a speck of manure here and there like raisins on a crust of bread.

As I toss about in my bed to fight the pains of aging, I return once more to my spirit symbols, those river images, to experience the real and natural things of long ago. It's always a pleasure to walk in the fields of wonder, that river country, before the coming of autumn. And revisit them in a spiritual form.

This place where wilderness speaks more truth than memory, it reaches out to lead me there with grass-stained hands. It will return again, no doubt, in some desolate moment of sleep.

River Home

Yes, this is my river, my home; the place of my birth and early life. Born and bred in sight of its waters, its woods and fields, I can tell you first-hand that my Miramichi has not been the stereotypical place of shameful drinking sprees, the frolicking log drivers, or the rowdy, dance-hall fisticuffs—the wild and woolly perception of so many from outside our region.

No, the Miramichi of my childhood was one of spending an evening at the river with school chums, where a salmon caught was divided between three families. Of hoeing my father's bean garden on the hottest days of summer, so the sun's heat on the unearthed roots would kill the weeds. Of long walks on quiet summer nights when the scent of cherry blossom purified the atmosphere. Of pitching straw from behind a rumbling oat-separator on the splintered thrashing floor of the barn. Of walking more than a kilometre to school on a highway of frozen shale—a slingshot, with many notches on its handle, in my pocket—while looking for partridge or squirrels in the woods along the way. Of new skates arriving, mail-order from Eaton's of Canada in late November, and the frosty evenings spent on the river ice while a burning car tire sent sparks scattering towards the heavens, a blaze that winked at us from a kilometre up the moonlit river. Of giving a hand as the team of horses and the bobsleds brought our stovewood from the forest on winter afternoons—princess pine stubs that I was responsible for sawing and splitting into kindling—to be carried into the kitchen where it dried in the stove's oven, filling the house with the sweet scent of violin rosin. Of the staticky radio shows—*Mark Trail*, *Gang Busters*, and *Boston Blackie*—when the evening's chores were finally done.

Of the Red Ryder, the Lone Ranger, and Superman comic books my brothers, sister, and I picked up for ten cents each at Underhill's Five-and-Dime Store in Blackville, read, and then traded among our friends. Of the singing cowboys Hank Snow, Johnny Cash, and Wilf Carter who came to the rink in town; their songs linger in my memory, "I've Been Everywhere," "Ballad of a Teenage Queen," "My Swiss Moonlight Lullaby." Of the black-and-white Westerns we went to see at the old church hall in Blackville on Saturday nights—Randolph Scott, Barbara Stanwyck, Guy Madison, their guns popping smoke, horses galloping in the one-on-one chase.

Of drawing aside the curtain on my bedroom window—using my palms to melt away the decorated patterns of frost—and watching the *Express* as it came down the tracks a little before midnight, its lighted coaches trailing across our top hill. And occasionally the headlamps that projected through the blowing snow, telling my brothers, sister, and me there would be no school tomorrow. Of the moving shadows that were thrown upon our trackless and snow-fenced dooryard—first in the front, then to the side, then in the back—as the dreary whistle sounded above the squeal of the iron wheels that scattered sparks into the snow as they idled down that long grade toward Newcastle. Of the tin horse-lanterns and harness bells of the ones who went to meet the train's arrival at the siding stop near home, the night winds making the snow drift along in the sleigh runners' sunken tracks.

I still have vivid memories of a long time ago—sixty years—and coming home on a winter evening to Keenan from Fredericton on the CNR *Express.* I was clasping the big green return ticket as I relaxed in the warm coach and stared out through the teary glass at the peacefulness of the snow-fallen countryside. I had spent a day in the city with my mother who was doing her Christmas shopping, last minute. And after experiencing Fredericton's hustle and bustle, I was happy to be boarding a train to head back "over north" to the freedom of the fields, woods, and frozen rivers and that magical world of my childhood, with its bows and arrows, slingshots, toy guns, and a Santa Claus that was still very real. Back to the river where life was genuine. And a whole lot more practical.

And I remember my great-aunts, Mary and Maggie, who in their generation's old-home tradition wrote to my grandmother (Barbie), every month for fifty years standing. Once a year, they came home from Houlton, Maine, in their 1938 Chevrolet coupe, which had a canvas top and a rumble seat. They were old ladies who spent their lifetimes in the USA but refused to become American citizens because they felt it would have been a betrayal of their patriotism to the home country. They had gone there as young women with their Miramichi husbands to work in the potato industry and having outlived these men by many years, stayed and worked their lives through. They came back to Blackville every summer until there was no Blackville—not the Blackville of their memories.

I can recall too, those blustery December evenings, standing before the fire in our wallpapered living room, which was filled with neighbours who applauded as my uncle Wilfred, a left-handed fiddler, played jigs and reels while my brother Gary stumbled to find the chords on the old keyboard. Darkness and snow were coming down outside as my mother, in her best dress, good-naturedly hurried about, serving homemade fruitcakes and tea in her finest china. And there was a great sense of humanness about so many twentieth-century souls sharing those poignant moments in time. They stood about like ceramic figurines in a display case, until, sensing it was late for them, Wilfred, like the hired violinist he professed to be—always independent because he had taken music lessons as a boy and was the only one in the community who could play—laid down his instrument and jokingly passed the hat. And then with a chorus of good nights and Merry Christmases everyone collected their coats and scarves and wandered off to their homes at half-past ten.

Those little house parties were the closest thing my mother ever had to romance. And it was there she practised the urbane etiquette she had been taught as a girl—cutlery that had to be laid out on the proper sides of the plates, the right wine glasses, the proper ways to fold a napkin, hold a tea cup—when she worked as a chambermaid in the Town of Newcastle and the City of Fredericton. Now it was at these Christmas functions that she appeared most happy, as if for the moment she was an aristocrat. Of course, she was always a lady in the eyes of her family and of the community. Self-contained and self-assured best describe her. She wore glasses that aged her by fifteen years, though she never took them off, and seldom if ever did she put on makeup. She would not waste good money on cosmetics.

And I believe it is through us, the country people, through these humble images, that the passing of time is measured, and indeed life's most dramatic changes have occurred. For all such traditions are now gone from this river. From the log hut that my great-great-grandfather built in 1818, to the socializing in Papa's farmhouse parlour, to the hospitality shown by a conductor on a passenger train, to the country songs we the river children sang during a sleigh ride, to the used Chevy half-ton my father bought in the spring of fifty-three. They remain only in memories and stand for a brief period in time as we travel between the eternities.

Yes, I am a part of that old day of unpretentious comforts, of fantastic dreams and old-world heroes and legends. Of the *Cisco Kid*, the *Six Shooter*, and *Sergeant Preston of the Yukon*. Of the 30-30 Winchester, with its full magazine, saddle ring, and Rocky Mountain sights, that my father carried under his arm when he hunted deer in the fall. Of the boxes of copper rifle bullets and the cases of paper shot-shells that stood on our dining-room table during the hunting season, the bone-handle hunting knives in leather sheaths we strapped to our belts.

Of the .38 Smith & Wesson revolvers worn on the hips of those tall Doaktown Mounties, who stopped at our place for a drink of hot tea, after helping Doctor Hamilton find his way across the river ice in a blizzard to deliver a baby for Mrs. Jardine. The late days of her pregnancy were a time when the community, so full of concern, was one big family.

People, young and old, struggled through the long hours of the workday and were content with the sacrifices they made, even revelled in the aches and pains of tired muscles at eventide, because it was considered a sacred thing to earn our keep by the sweat of our brows. And we were proud when the season's work was complete because the family had once again pulled together religiously in a united cause.

And I can remember how great the farm looked in the late summer, after the hay had been cut right up to the hawthorn-bushed line fences and down to the water's edge, and the after-grass had turned the stubble fields and the shores green once more. Yes, even as children we felt a sense of pride in this.

I can still see the images as clearly as if I'm looking into a barbershop mirror: the sunburned and weathered faces of my brothers after a day in the fields or woods; my sister stumbling in the lane behind the cows; my mother hanging clothes on a line that stretched across the dooryard on wooden pulleys that would not turn; my father, in his sweat-stained straw hat, pitching hay into the rung-rack of the truck-wagon while the horses kept it moving forward; and how the success of their labour was being threatened by an approaching thundercloud, its low, troubled skies looking like the wavering brush strokes of a Van Gogh landscape.

And there were paintings by Grandma Moses, poems by Robert Frost. The studded-harness teams of draft horses, the cedar rail fences at the edges of pastures. The sodden fields on days of November rain, the silent woods of an approaching winter, the spring pools where trout snapped at my baited hook after the sun went down.

In my Miramichi, those inspirational moments were as innocent and consoling as the Sunday school hymns I sang as a child. Or the laughter that my brothers and sister and I shared as we played our little games of fox and geese on the new and untracked snow of early winter. Or the joyousness we had in common as we stood by my mother's upright piano and sang her favourite hymns "Abide with Me" and "In the Garden," a tradition without which a New Brunswick Sunday would not have been the Sabbath at all.

I am aware that it was my generation, in good part, that let that old world die. And it's not without shame that I recall, all too vividly, the quarrels I had with my father (such a kind man too) before I quit school for keeps and left the river early in the fall of 1962.

I had reached the age when I no longer agreed with very much that he said, and itching for excitement and a new direction, I hitchhiked to Upper Canada, where I found work in a car factory. Yes, the autumn I was nineteen, I left my father to work alone in the fields and woods, a move that would have been considered a disgrace in any rural community, for he was not a young man then, and it was understood that the older sons of the household would stay to help raise and educate the siblings.

And I remember those lonesome, hungry nights, sleeping in an old car on the beaches of Lake Ontario. Of trying to adapt to the social cliques, the union mentality, the tedium of factory work and night shift in the industrial heartland of our country. It was a thing that should never have happened, could never have happened, not successfully, not to the kind of country homebody that I was. I can see it now as I think of the words from Wallace Stegner's *Angle of Repose*:

> Home is a notion that only the nations of the homeless fully appreciate and only the uprooted comprehend.... What else would one plant in a wilderness...? What loss would hurt more?

And it makes me melancholy to think that when I returned to the river to live a few years later, the old farmstead as I remembered it was already a thing of the past. The livestock and the horse machinery had been sold, the outbuildings torn down, and the fields were growing up in alder and spruce. My father was keeping only a small garden because it cost less to buy a side of pork or a can of beans at the supermarket than it did to grow them on the farm. The young men and women of my age group would not stay home and work the long hours that farm life required of them, as our grandparents and parents had done for so many years. And because of this, the community had all but vanished. And this had happened not only in my old home region but also in rural settlements right across our land. Indeed for the country people, during the sixties, for better or worse, there had been a real-life revolution, an urbanization of all our rural communities.

Still, by then, due to new social programs and government pensions, for the first time my parents were watching a colour television, driving a good car, and heating their house with furnace oil. Yes, they had found a bit of comfort, finally. Financially, at least, they were better off than they had ever been and with fewer worries because now there were doctors and social workers and caretakers to help and support them. No longer did they have to work—as my grandfathers had done—until they were almost a hundred years old to keep the family farm. No longer did they have to suffer illnesses because they couldn't afford to go to a doctor. No longer did the oldest son have to quit school to help his parents support his younger brothers and sisters. In the evenings and on weekends, instead of working in the fields or the woods, they took their fly rods and headed for the river to enjoy a few hours of angling, just as the rich people from away—who had bought up most of our best fishing pools for little or no money because we had been hard up—had been doing for years. Yes, the urban lifestyle had made its way into our countryside; the days of the family farm on this river were already being spoken of in the past tense.

But while my father may have gone along with these changes, it was not without some resentment toward me because I didn't stay and help him keep the old way going. Working the farm, river, and woods was what he knew best and what had made him whole. While conceding to the leisure, even boredom, of the new lifestyle, he still carried inside him a belief that what he was saving in time and labour, he was losing in self-respect, even dignity—from the rest of the family and from the community—and in his own sense of self-importance. He lamented the losses, both physical and spiritual, of the healthier lifestyle, and he struggled with the realization that not even a chicken or a calf depended on him for anything. And always with a longing for the simple pleasures of watching his cream go to market, his grain fields ripening before the fall harvest, and his own brand of potatoes being tasted at the church supper in the village. While this was never spoken about, we could see it in him. He carried a yearning for the old world, along with a pathetic sense of being an alien in the new.

For my mother, it had been different: the country had meant nothing to her but misery and hardship, and as the times changed for the better, she never looked back or longed for the past. In truth, I believe she would have left the country long before, had she another place to go.

My father lived to be ninety-four years old, and the last ten years of his life he was a stranger in an even stranger land. My brothers, sister, and I had tried to ease his inability to change from the old ways. So did my mother. And we secretly hoped that the country of our time would never see us get so old, so deep-rooted in a single way of life that we could not adapt.

But my father saw this appeasement in those of us around him, even as we fly-fished our home pool (which is still in the family), barbecued salmon over hardwood coals on the shore, smoked one cigarette after another, and toasted the old man with accolades for the hard life he had experienced during his many years on the farm, in the woods, and at the river.

Or when, wearing a touch of orange, we sat on a log beside a fire in the woods, drank a toast to the new-growth trees, and reminisced about his many days as a lumberman, a farmer, and a river guide. On those dark days of late November, our little fire lit up an otherwise drab forest, its smells and tastes carrying the most memorable images to him. (He had spent so many of his early years in the lumber woods.) This day, we had gone there as an excuse to look for a Christmas tree, so far from home that the only earthly sounds were the squawk of ravens or the chirp of a Canada jay (a bird of good omen that ate from our palms), or the trickle of Morse Brook that flowed through our otherwise silent woods. At outings like this my father would sip Scotch and ramble on about his good-times past, the lumbering, the log driving, the hunting, and the river guiding. And even though he was by then a phantom of nostalgia who was repeating himself, and repeating himself, his tired old voice was a pleasure to hear.

Yes, we listened, and we listened, as he grasped backwards for his youth. Though not really a drinking man, at parties he indulged with us, to the point where my mother would scold him, take his glass away. And she scolded his sons and daughter for giving him liquor. At such times he would join in the folk music of our time, take part in our hootenannies. (In his early years he had sung country songs in the logging camps and on the river drives.) But we knew he was singing with us only to try to fit in, to make the world come just a bit closer to what his heart actually desired—the good old days. And he did most of this at the river, out of the view of my mother's caring eyes. For the river was something that had not changed in our lives, and remains even now a getaway for us all. Yes, we were all river people, first and last. We shared that common thread, and this could not have changed, even though it was obvious to those of us who knew Daddy that he was living in the distant past and that the river and fly-fishing had by then become his exile.

I can remember, too, how difficult it was for him to have to release his first big salmon after angling with me for an afternoon in June. "We're just wasting our time out here then," he said. "Catching fish and letting them go again!"

Indeed, for him, the times were a-changing for the worse, and he was frustrated because there just wasn't anything that he could do to swing it all around. "The country's all gone to hell!" he said once as we stood and looked at a train whistle-post that was smothered by the trees, the tracks having long been dismantled. "The goddamn government!"

Of course, he was too old to be transplanted, too set in his ways to adapt anywhere else, as his sons and daughter were more able to do. In his declining days, he stood before an easel and sketched the farm and river scenes of his early years, which—distorted by time and emotion—were always out of perspective. (They were entitled "The Threshing Barn," "The Wood Cutters," "The Hay Load," "The Plowed Fields," "The Log

Jam," "The Leaping Salmon.") It was as if he felt that the hour of truth—the best years of his life—had to be told before the hour of his death, even though it was a brush stroke wherein the subject matter always outweighed the art. Daddy was not a great artist and his paintings were valuable only to those of us who loved him.

When my mother died, my father was completely lost without her. He sat in his rocking chair for hours and stared into space like a figure in meditation. "She's a sad old world," he would say.

My father died in June 2004, but his mind and spirit had stopped functioning long before that. I can remember visiting him in an extended care unit where he was tied to a chair, diapered, his pajamas falling down. Clutching a handkerchief, he dabbed his leaky eyes as he repeated the question, "Who the hell are you? Whose boy are ya anyway?" And I had to shout my name in his ear, because he had become so hard of hearing. And of course he was singing, always singing some old cowboy ditty from his youth. As far as I am concerned, they could have written on his tombstone that he was "Undone by the loss of his old way of life."

And because my mother had preceded him to the grave, our farmhouse was then closed up—like so many along this river had been before it.

Today, these experiences, these places and times, all of which are in the mind, are the most valuable things in our lives and are there for all the river people. They cannot be stolen by governments or given away to foreigners by any one of us. And, like the heartfelt memories of our vanished communities, they are still a big part of my internal landscape and are certainly not for sale.

Wisdom, as Stegner put it, is knowing what you have to accept.

But I am my grandfather's and father's son in that regard.

Public Water

Through the late seventies and the eighties, when the first bright salmon came in from the sea, my brothers, sister, and I angled the public waters. On weekends during the months of June and July, we left home in that first light before sunrise to go to those great, fast-water pools, without shame, ahead of the anglers from outside our river community; even though we felt there was a certain disgrace that came to long-standing river people who ended up fly-fishing in such places. These old pools—and indeed the farms they belonged to—had been lost, for whatever reason, by our fellow river families, many of which were our uncles, aunts, or cousins.

We drove our old pickup trucks or open Jeeps over kilometres of dusty or mud-greased roads to pools along the open-water stretches of the Miramichi and her tributaries. And I can still feel the bounce and heave of the four-wheel-drive on those abandoned logging trails that ran forever through woods of poplar and birch. It loosened our joints and made our heads ache, while the slap of brambles tilted our side mirrors, and the bracken that smothered the wheel wounds hid the stumps and granite rocks that popped up and dented our oil pans.

We made our way out onto the river flats where the giant elm trees cast their blue morning shadows across short-growth fields, still called by their family names—the old Johnston place, the Teedelin place, the Andy Porter (my great-uncle's) place—a century after their people had vacated those remote parts of our province forever. On those old-world homesteads, it was easy to stumble upon a crumbling rock cellar, a windmill skeleton, or a piece of rusted horse machinery abandoned in some overgrown corner of what had once been a hayfield or an oat field.

On farms less remote, like the old Foran place on the Little Southwest, the Colepaugh place on the Renous, or the Brophy place on the Cains, the grey-shingled farmhouses were still standing, their ivied verandas pitched forward onto the ground, gauze curtains flapping from upstairs windows without a wind, like white flags of surrender or the long dress trains of abandoned brides.

Only the birds of the sky, a few wild apple or plum blossoms, or perhaps a morning glory vine clinging to some rock stood as witness to what had once been a vibrant home and a farm community. And it was not hard to visualize the pain and the heartfelt loss that its people—their names are legendary on this river—must have suffered, having paid the ultimate price for having lived too long for a single ideal, the vanished dreams of clearing more land, plowing and harrowing more fields, planting grain all the way from the river to the railway line, a distance of eighty rods, and replenishing the horse machinery to be passed down to the next of kin.

Because of their remoteness and the trends toward urbanization in the mid-decades of the last century, those old farmsteads (my own home among them) and that way of life died in the spiritless winds of government promise and false hope. And I was sure that if I stood awhile and listened to the silences, I could have heard the tinkling of cowbells on the river flats, the clomping of the horses' hoof irons as they pranced upon the scattered fieldstones, and the grinding of spoked wheels on the hay-laden truck-wagons as they rattled along those rocky lanes. Or possibly the more delicate sounds of the single wagon wheels, cutting along a wood track, as sand poured through the spokes, while a young mare paced in stride as Uncle Jack and Aunt Lillian, sitting upright and proper in their best Sunday clothes, left the farm to attend a church service in that little three-windowed, clapboard chapel that stood near the forks in the road, or to go instead to the one-room school where Aunt Lillian taught for most of her life. Jack drove her to and from work in that buggy, or in the winter, a horse-drawn sleigh. Later, he travelled in a Model A Ford, which he had to crank to get started and which had a square roof and duck-quack horn.

I can remember my despair at seeing an aging neighbour or uncle having to sell his way of life and close down his farm because of the lack of young legs to help keep it all going, and for money enough to retire in a nursing home. We, the younger generation, had by then discovered—perhaps through television—new dreams and new ambitions; we wanted to move on to a more exciting lifestyle. And the beckoning whistles of the freight and passenger trains that eventually took us all away from there are echoed now in the yellow-throated warbler's "witchie, witchie, witchie" and the ovenbird's "teacher, teacher, teacher." Those invisible birds call to one another from the trees, their repetitious little songs carrying the images of that old place and time right through the never-ending summers.

To me, the saddest thing in the world is a "For Sale" sign on a centuries-old farmhouse or a river cottage. Like an empty bed, it is symbolic of a love, a dream, or a way of life gone sour.

Indeed those old farms, and as a consequence their home fishing pools—where the white shore gravel turned copper under the currents, and the Atlantic salmon, the most sought-after game fish in the world, leaped forward on their way upstream to spawn—in many cases became waters that had been returned to the hands of governments because of back taxes. Or perhaps they had been sold to foreigners, early on, for the fishing rights (for one-tenth of their market value) when money was needed to put a bathroom or a chimney in the farmhouse, or perhaps to purchase a good second-hand car. Many more pools were lost due to the failure of their disheartened owners—who had been the life of the farm but had grown too old to do the work—to make a will. Or maybe river ownership had never been negotiated in the fine print by its grantors when some of those farms were settled long ago. For such documents were not necessary in those early days of plenty. And of course, the owners had no idea as to the value of what their frontages would be worth years later.

Whatever the reason, some of those old home waters—the ones that had not been sacrificed to pay for illness or taxes—had been taken over by the government for the purpose of allowing the people of the province a place to fish. It was public water and kept available to us all.

And the people from outside our river came in their four-wheel-drive Jeeps hauling tin trailers. And their pickup trucks with the box-shaped campers idled along carelessly onto the property and across the old fields to stake out a campsite for the summer, where they drank beer, partied, and fished without knowing the water's history or caring a damn. For only the local people worried about such trivial things, they said.

At some of these pools, the local river people had to stand in line in a slow rotation, waiting to take our turn angling—down through the waters that we had once owned—behind an arrogant gaggle of unfriendly casters from God knows where, people who had spent the night on the property and were dressed and on the water at the first light of morning. These were people who had no understanding of our river and its families' connections. Nor did they know or attempt to exercise the proper stream etiquette. Iron-faced, they stood in armoured clothing, so deep in the water they looked like the busts of chessmen as they moved, or didn't move—to allow a proper rotation—through the pool. Their quizzical eyes destroyed everything the river or the thrill of angling should have stood for. For they were also taxpayers, they said, and residents of this province, and as such, they had the right to angle in any government or disputed water they stumbled upon, regardless of its history. Rocks were thrown and fist fights erupted. In the parking areas, car tires were slashed and gas tanks were filled with sugared water.

It was classified as combat fishing.

Angling or attempting to angle the waters that had been purchased by non-resident anglers for whatever reason was a similar experience, though less combative. While most of these people were kind and left the local people alone, especially after they themselves had gone back home, some kept their property posted, their gates locked, and sometimes a surveillance camera was installed so they could sit in their offices in Montreal or New York and keep an eye on their river property. If they saw someone in the pool, or even in the field or on the riverbank, they called the local caretaker to look after things. Many of these people, especially the ones from the big corporations employed a full-time warden to police their waters. And I can tell you as a seventh-generation son-of-the-river witnessing the outsider (provincial or otherwise) take over our river in that fashion was like watching the new lover making-out with your ex-wife. It was not easy to smile and bear it.

Of course this led to vandalism. "No Trespassing" signs were chucked into the river, boats were set adrift in the night, and in the off-season cabins were burned to the ground.

The Mounties were called in. These men and women came to the scene wearing their high brown boots, britches, and fur caps with the big buffalo badges. They stood and chucked snowballs into the fire, as they asked question after question after question. "Who would do such a thing? And why?" They didn't know the river's history; they didn't know the heart of the matter because they were also from somewhere else. The local men and women came to their windows—with babies in their arms—to witness the approaching authorities. The Mounties knocked on many doors and got few answers. Finally they drove away with the understanding that, "Nobody didn't see nothin'."

When I was a schoolboy in the early fifties, the fishing hole at my grandfather's and father's farm produced bright salmon only when the river was high and cold, and the fish were moving through. Or in September/October, when the Cains River salmon run was held up in front of home, waiting for the water in that tributary to rise so they could make it over the shallows to their spawning beds. (Our place was less than two kilometres below the mouth of the Cains River.)

My grandparents, and to a lesser degree my parents, had speared and netted these salmon for the salt barrels, but in my own time, my brothers, sister, and I fly-fished. Angling after school and on weekends each autumn, we brought home enough salmon to be salted for the winter's food supply. We found that those big fall hook-bills would take a fly hook on the first cast, and we spent many hours on the river.

In the summer, our pool became very warm and it was a

good place to swim and sail and test our car-tube rafts. Until the dog days of August came and we were instructed by parents to stay away from the river because of the threat of smallpox and polio and other life-threatening diseases that were said to be in the water, and which only a rainstorm of biblical proportions could purify.

Decades before this, other more productive summer pools along the main river were purchased for very little money by non-residents who knew the real value of a piece of waterfront, the-not-so-subtle riffs and foam lines where an Atlantic salmon could be taken with the cast of a fly hook even in the heat of summer. These fast-flowing, low-water pools were—they had been told—the better fish-holding waters. And, of course, they were.

My grandfather told me that as a young man, he sold many tons of gravel from the beach in front of our place, when the government was building a bridge across Morse Brook just downriver from home. He said the construction crews trucked all summer, until what might have been a great salmon pool was reduced to a "shad hole" for a few cents a truck-wagon load.

I suppose I should not criticize Papa for his short-sightedness, as he was trying to feed a family of twelve, and, back then, a salmon could be taken for the spearing or the netting anywhere along that stretch of river below the mouth of the Cains, which non-resident anglers now call the Golden Horseshoe. In Papa's time, water was shared by all farmers and woodsmen equally.

But I always felt that, if our pool had been more consistent in its salmon catches, if Papa had not sold that gravel, or if the would-be buyers had had a greater knowledge of the species they were after, or indeed were anglers who could have learned how to fish the slow water, our place would have been gone, too, with perhaps fishing rights reserved for the immediate family. For there were illnesses, taxes to be paid, chimneys and a bathroom to be installed in our farmhouse, too. And some of these quandaries were expensive: my aunt Lillian had spent twenty years in a sanatorium, and there had been the death of her brother and sister before they reached their teen years; the tax man was paid next; and the luxuries of having things like a bathroom were done without until I was almost grown up. But I am thankful now that my grandfather and father loved the farm as they did, a farm that included the river.

Papa's actions at the shore could never be reversed. In the eighties my brothers, sister, and I acquired a permit from the Department of Natural Resources to install boulders and build piers in the home pool. With government supervision, trucks and bucket loaders were used to place big rocks at angles here and there in the pool to increase the water's speed and create more oxygen for the fish to breathe. We gave a whole new meaning to the phrase "riparian rights." But the pool never regained its previous potential, and today life goes on pretty much as it did sixty years ago. We talk of permits and boulders, and how to restore Papa's beach, which might take a billion years to do naturally, if ever. And while we wait—during the low-water seasons—we fish the public water.

Still, we are grateful that the old man had the foresight to have written a will, to have kept the farm and especially the home pool in the family, however inconsistently it fished. And that my father did not follow a pattern that so many along the river had set and sell the shore when times got tough. For it was a beautiful stretch of river frontage, where we, the sons and daughter, would eventually build our own cabins.

Yes, it was good that we still had our part of the river to share, along with the public waters, however unfriendly they had become. But make no mistake: the Miramichi of my parents' years and even my grandparents' years, say from the early 1900s to the 1970s, was already being claimed, in good part, by people in Geneva, London, New York, Montreal, and Hamburg.

While these outsiders had acquired deeds and built cottages on some of our best river places, and we were forced to go to the open water to catch a fish at certain times of the summer, we still had the river itself, which continued to flow among its own people. It is said that you can buy a river, but you can't take it home with you.

On the Cains

A long-standing tradition for the people of Miramichi is an annual canoe trip down the lower stretches of our biggest tributary, the Cains. This one-day journey was something I had not done since my sons were small, but which the boys and I had been trying to organize for a long time. It was not easy to get so many busy people to commit to this kind of time in this modern day. But it finally came together in the summer of 2000.

The day began early with Jeff, Jason, and Steven arriving here at the old camp shortly after dawn. At six o'clock we drank coffee; Jason cooked breakfast while I made arrangements for the canoe rentals. We set out for Shinniks Burn by Jeep, travelling fourteen kilometres in two vehicles. The old launching area at the Moore's is, as the crow flies, ten kilometres from the mouth of the Cains and almost twenty by river. It's a full day's run back to our place in the best water conditions.

It was Saturday, June 28.

Already, so early in the day, it was hot, but the Cains had a cool, morning smell. And there was that unique atmosphere that always signifies this river as a state of mind, a state of soul, more than just a place. The sun, having already penetrated a ghostly fog, had burned away the froth that raced in the channels by the time we pushed off. We paddled with vigour, down on the currents, riding high on the thwarts, ducking under sweeps that shaded the water—there would be trout in places like that—and steering with the best of skills around rocks where the water broke into choppy white curls of turbulence. In the bends, we edged close to ledges and the bear-shaped boulders. It was like sitting in a movie house, watching a huge screen while zooming down a river, the freshet sounds sometimes overpowering our conversation. We rested here and there in a bend to escape the sun, which by midday was splitting rocks.

We canoed over salmon pools such as the School House, Cashin's, the Oxbow, Pigeon Ledge, and the mouth of the Sabbies. In some of these places, the water was so smooth we could see the reflection of shoreline trees, greenery projecting downward toward an underwater sky, sun clouds on the bottom, the surface wrinkled only by the strokes of our paddles, which sent little curls spinning behind the boats.

We navigated through that long stretch of slow water, how long it was yet, with our eagerness, how fast it all was left behind. "Be happy, have a good day," the breezy elm trees whispered above us. We hooded our eyes to see the washed gravel that moved backwards under the boats, the sun burning our faces and bare arms in spite of the sunscreen lotion we had rubbed into our skin.

For a short distance, a mother merganser with a brood of

ducklings nervously scampered along ahead of us. Half flying, half swimming, they eventually skidded to a refuge where some willow shrubs hung over the river. And there was a gulping sound as the heavy water frothed over a big rock. For an instant I thought of a day when the boys were small. We had been paddling along, singing, when our canoe struck that rock and we almost capsized. The incident frightened them so badly, they wanted to go ashore and walk back to camp. Later on that trip, because it had started to rain, we had lunch in a cave just across the river from the Herman Campbell camp. But this day we lunched at my great-uncle Andy Porter's place, just below Salmon Brook. (His rock cellar is still visible.) I lay down to rest on an old cow path where the new leaves of a poplar tree rattled overhead, even without a breeze, and the sun made broken patches of yellow on the ground. From here the river made no sound. My sons made tea, which was not bad tasting in spite of the barren-fed water and the tin pan in which it was brewed. After lunch, I spent some time wandering about the hillside looking for flowers from Grammy Porter's old garden. I found black-eyed Susan that would have been planted almost two centuries before.

"Your great-great-grandmother was born and raised on this farm," I told the boys. And for a split second I could see Maggie Porter on wash days, as she carried water from the river to her house in two iron-banded wooden buckets. Gram's portrait now hangs in the old farmstead in Keenan. In an oval frame, she sits on a tufted chair in a fancy dress, a rose at her bosom. And because this is the only likeness we have of her, she appears to me in that dress and with that same delicate smile, here now.

A cock-of-the-woods screamed from a poplar corpse.

Here, the riverscape, along with the voices of nature, give me a tendency to brag about the family's river posterity. It always did. And I commence to ramble a bit. I tell the boys that our family has been rooted on this river for generations; that my grandfather had a log cabin just down around the bend at the Buttermilk Brook Landing; it was a logging and caribou camp, and like its reasons for being here, it is long gone. I also had an uncle, Silas, who moved here to live when he married in the 1920s. He raised a large family near the schoolhouse where Aunt Lillian taught for many terms; she was a consumptive woman, even in her early years, and would spend much of her life in a sanatorium. Her husband, Jack Underwood, perished here on a log drive. It was the spring of 1953, when I was in grade four, but I remember it well; the dark days out of school, the big military funeral, the aunt who came back home to live.

And when this farm and others were abandoned, for a time afterwards, the fields were referred to as the Commons. It was a place for farmers from along the main river to bring their cattle to graze for the summer. They would tent in an elm grove on the river flats and harvest the shore hay.

For the everyday angler, these people and places are now identified with salmon pools, but I speak of them as old relations. When I come here I can feel them, and I'm moved by my own modest notions of posterity. But my boys have heard all this before, every time we paddle down this river. They appear unimpressed, even bored. Still whenever we are canoeing, we talk about rivers and river people and how the two are connected. We are all related in this way, drawn together by the streams that flow inside us. But for us the Cains holds a strong family tie. I can see this more and more in my sons as they grow older. They canoe here on their own and sometimes they bring a group of friends and make the run.

After lunch, Steven cast a small dry-fly across water that seemed to be swirling from out of a ledge. I saw a splash at his hook and watched as he cranked in a smolt-size speckled trout, its orange belly flashing under the surface, the line thumping against the spring and bounce of the lifted rod. He cast again and again without another rise, and then we had to move on.

We drifted over salmon pools called Buttermilk Brook, the Long Hole, Long Hole Rapids, Slide Pool, Hydro Pool, and Brophy's Brook, where through Polaroid sunglasses we saw a hen salmon resting but did not cast because the water temperatures exceeded twenty degrees; we did not want to stress her. We continued past Hooper's and Duffy's Run. These waters harbour the big, kype-faced hook-bills of autumn, speckled with a camouflage of orange and autumnal browns. They become antagonistic and territorial as spawning time approaches and will often snap at a fly on impulse.

Ahead of us we could see a cliff and the steep, pine-treed hillsides and knew there was a sharp bend in the river and, consequently, faster water. We clasped our paddles and in an adrenalin rush, faced into Hell's Gates Rapids, where the boat bounced and swayed and bucked as we busily steered around the gulping underwater boulders that could have tossed us all into the frothing river to be swept away like matchsticks.

As the day got hotter and the sun hammered down on the

boat, I had an urge to jump overboard. We paddled to shore and drank from one of the small tributaries, where the water was so cold it made our teeth ache. And there was, as always, that smell I could taste, the scent of hawthorn and wild cherry blossom, of shore grass and beaver kill, of washed gravel, dried by the sun.

A beaver lodge with new works stood at the edge of an eddy, and there was a sad encampment, like something out of Joseph Conrad's *Heart of Darkness*—a tin-roofed shed, with a slanting flag pole and sunken woodpile, abandoned years before because of a land squabble. For a moment our chatter drifted to literature—to Conrad and his characters Marlow and Kurtz. Jeff said, "Oh the horror! The horror!" Then the conversation led to the sensuous dream rivers in the *Arabian Nights*, with a brief look at Tennyson, before we delved into Chekhov, Tolstoy, and Proust, until this river, the Cains—where we saw a doe and two fawns drinking from a spring on the shore—brought us back to reality. Not hard to get carried away in a place like that.

A porcupine hobbled up the bank.

Our second lunch was at Brophy's, a small island at the foot of Hell's Gates. We wolfed down our submarine sandwiches and juices. And then, tired from the early start and the exposure, we took a half-hour break. We sat in the lee of a cool sod-and-gravel embankment with our bare feet in the water and listened to the sounds of the wilderness. It's wonderful how one loses track of the hours when on a river. It has to be the best escape there is when it comes to blocking out the wrath of modern life. We could have sat there for hours but knew we had to move on.

We wanted to get back to camp, the boys having made plans for the evening.

We rested our paddles across the gunwales and let the water carry us until we could see open farmlands and cultivation, the changing hues of the hillsides, and the tall shore grasses as they shifted in the hot, upriver breezes. All this gave a quaint and melancholy air to the little community of Howard, which sits on a bluff where the Cains enters into the Miramichi. And there was the ever-present chatter from the sport fishers in the big salmon pools below the forks.

An aged horse stood beneath an oak tree, cow herds by the river, distant farmhouses painted white, a little mission church (Our Lady of Mount Carmel), its steeple reaching above a canopy of spruce toward Heaven, the little clapboard houses in proximity like goslings around a mother goose. They shift their positions and their spirits in sequence to the moving canoe. And there were the funeral grounds nestled upon a hill, their gravestones (so intimate in nature) near the one-room schoolhouse, which so many in my age group had attended, some of whom I helped carry to their graves. For an instant I heard the funeral hymn "Ave Maria" and the Holy Liturgy read in the baritone voice of Father Vincent Donovan. These things kept repeating themselves, as we paddled beyond the mission district, toward where our home cabin stands. The sounds grew faint above the warble of birds, the trickle of water. We moved along, leaving the little church as quiet as if it had not seen us, with its stained glass windows and single spire, standing against the receding sun, as though listening to the constant sounds of the river.

Further down, we passed the Charlie Hague property—purchased from my uncle Eldon more than five decades ago—where only a sketch of its fireplace chimney remained, the place having burned to the ground on a December day in the early sixties, they say, after the New York family kindled a blaze in the hearth and left the cabin to go skating on the river ice. Later, from a far bend they saw smoke and hurried back to a building already engulfed in flames. The cabin was never restored, and the owner, because of these memories, did not return.

My son Jeff now owns that property, having purchased it from an American, fifty-odd years after it left the family's possession. I counted at least six rock chimneys that peeked at us from among the trees that day. These Hansel and Gretel–like structures stood as monuments that bore witness to the cabins and dreams—of a more innocent time—taken down for whatever reason. I could say that elves put them there. But like Robert Frost, I'd rather the reader saw that for themselves. We paddled against an upriver breeze through lengthening shadows. A few minutes more and we were downloading at the camp.

The trip had been wonderful from the start. It would be hard not to have a good time with that company, on that river, on a day like that. I knew my sons shared these feelings, but the words were never spoken, rather understood, as if our enjoyment from the experience could have been lost if it was talked about.

River Legacy

The Child is father of the Man;
And I could wish my days to be
Bound each to each by natural piety.

William Wordsworth,
"My Heart Leaps Up"

When my sons were young I took them with me wherever I went. We flew kites, played golf and tennis, and in the fall we hunted birds. It was impossible to go to the river or a trout stream without them. It seems we were always together, and happy. To be sure, the experiences I encountered on those outings of long ago nourish my soul even to this day.

At the shore in front of our cabin, all four of us would crowd into my old square-stern canoe, and the boys kept seated while I poled upriver and dropped the anchor in a place from where each of us could reach the middle bar with a cast. And we took turns flailing the water in rotation. With so many flylines being thrown, so many separate presentations being offered, so much anticipatory restitution being speculated from one boat, it was not easy to keep things from snarling, literally.

But even in the boys' early years, each one had his own tackle. These ranged from an eight-foot fibreglass two-piece

Shakespeare rod that my father had been given by baseball player Ted Williams years before, which Steven used until he was almost grown up; to an old Fenwick graphite eight-footer given to me by my father as a birthday gift in the sixties, which had been adopted by Jason; to a nine-foot, two-inch boron Eagle hand-me-down that I had had rebuilt by a friend not long before she died in the mid-seventies, which I had given to Jeff as a Christmas gift; to a nine-foot Orvis—we are now Orvis people—I had saved my writing money to buy and which I still use. Indeed, those rods were a collection of memorabilia that carried the values of our home, river, and growing family.

It was very much my river in those days: my river, my equipment, and my technique. Because I had been taught by my father, as he had been taught by his. And of course having grown up on these waters, and having used them as a source of livelihood, I knew all river and earthly things better than my children were expected to at their ages. By their time, we had grown to be less reliant on the river as a place to find a bite to eat. And, going back, this was also the case between the time of my river days and those of my father, whose equipment had been antique in comparison to mine, as was his methodology, which carried in it an atmosphere of earlier, harder times, and a great deal more dependency upon the waters he fished. In my grandfather's day, spears and nets were used to bring salmon to our kitchen tables. My father's early fishing rods were made of split bamboo and steel with level casting lines and catgut leaders that had to be soaked before a fly hook could be tied on. Those old Scots pattern flies were made from a variety of exotic feathers. And it was believed that each feather carried an equal importance. It was almost impossible to cast them satisfactorily, especially in the wind.

But I could sense, even when my sons were angling with me, my methods and my advice on equipment would also be a short-lived study, because technology was changing faster than I was ever capable of doing. In fact, in some cases, the boys were teaching their mother and father how to communicate in the modern, electronic age.

In later years, when my sons took me fishing with them on Father's Day, it had long since become their river: their river, their equipment, and their technique. This was something never spoken of, rather it was felt, if not completely understood, by me. Or perhaps even by them, because it was in a slow and subtle manner that it came about. For sure, they had respectfully surpassed me in their sophisticated presentations of fly and line, and of course they had outgrown my other childish entertainments long before that.

The equipment, such as boats, paddles, wading boots, and clothing had also changed. Again. The quality of fishing tackle, like all technology, had been revolutionized during the boys' early years as well, so that they had grown with the changes and understood the new equipment and proficiency it required much better than I ever would. Like the modern-day equipment that golfers use wherein the old golf courses have to be redesigned to make them a bit more challenging. Like so many things that are mysterious and inaccessible to me about the so-called age of information. It's all a kind of blur.

The impressions that one has later in life, I suspect, are no longer original, or even positive, but rather cynical toward all forms of modernization and innovation. So that my sons no longer sought my advice on anything, river or, for that matter, non-river related.

And I felt this in the patience, or lack of patience, they showed toward their aging father, whose head was white—like the snow on top of a park statue—and who was limping slightly from sore bones, as they helped me get into a life jacket and then get seated on a cushion in the bow of a canoe, or in the tying of a wading staff to the loop in my fishing vest. Or just offering me an arm or a shoulder to lean on as I waded into those slippery bottom, fast-water pools around home.

"Be careful now Dad," they would say. "Don't fall."

By this time in our lives, due to our social programs, plus the conservation practices being enforced due to the depletion of the fish stocks, the river itself had come to represent something different as well. For the river people, it was no longer regarded as a partner in the never-ending struggles for survival—at least not in the bring-home-a-fish-for-the-table sense of the word—except perhaps for the income earned in guiding or accommodating river enthusiasts from elsewhere.

Nor were the new breed of so-called river people deep-rooted. No, these were the more transient, part-time cottage souls who lived away, and worked away, and were certainly not depending on the stream as a source of livelihood; rather, it had become a place of recreation or amusement. So the river meant less to them when it came to heart or true gut-feelings. The old perceptions of looking at the stream, like we did the land, as a part of the rural soul had also vanished. And for the folks who had lived on this river for generations, families for whom the river had been considered sacred, if not holy, the new river people brought with them attitudes of sacrilege. For they had no feelings for the water as anything other than a place to party. It's like watching someone pick the blossoms from your apple orchard, arrange them in a decorative vase without adding water to keep them from wilting while expecting apples to be on that tree come fall.

But this transition did not come about until after my sons had grown up on the river, had heard the respectful accounting of former times—not that long ago in calendar years—and had participated in a few experiences themselves. Of course, the stream had been flowing in their veins for two centuries, so they loved the river life as I did.

When the boys were small we had canoed many rivers together and cast our fly hooks over waters that I can now only fantasize about getting to, except perhaps in my dreams, or in my fading, though increasingly glorified memory. And we killed fish and ate them a dozen different ways. These fish were actually needed as a source of food, while the days were uncertain and often wearisome, and while we were striving to get into a position to be where we are today (financially healed so that we no longer have to kill anything to survive), I can say without a hint of nostalgia that those days were among the very best of my life; although, I didn't realize it at the time. As if the long-range pursuit of what we were going after was more important than its acquisition. There is an old saying that goes, essentially, "a man does not value his greatest moments until they are a long way behind him." Indeed, those have become days to be relived time and time again, enjoyed, even lauded as the years pass.

There is also a side of me from those years that I am really ashamed of. And this feeling is nourished by the sense of recklessness, even foolhardiness that came with the hunger I had for high adventure back then. I was never as careful in avoiding calamity or as protective of my sons' safety as today's more sophisticated parents are with their young, either on the river or in a convertible Jeep that I drove through woods too fast and without wearing a seat belt. Even now, so many years later, these images return in dreams to haunt me.

Once, I remember, when the boys and I were fishing grey trout in Long Lake, our lives were threatened. It was on the long weekend in May and so cold there were still patches of snow under the trees at the lakeshore. Using spoons and spinners, we were well out into the depths, trolling—the compound is fifteen kilometres long—when a windstorm came up and it took all the strength and boat savvy I had to, ever so carefully, swing the rented craft around in the two-metre waves and head back to camp. As I turned the boat slowly in the cross-chop, water splashed in over the gunwale, and I could see a bouldered shoreline and a sharp ledge that would have splintered our little punt into shreds had the motor shut off. And yes, we were out there without life jackets; so stupid. I have had a fear of lakes ever since, and sometimes even now I wake up in the night, screaming for the children to sit low in the boat and "Hang on!"

Another time I spent a full day adrift on Lake Ontario, after rowing out of Port Dalhousie—to look for ducks—with some friends from North Bay. A wind came up and we were unable to make it back to shore until the weather calmed. After sundown.

When you grow up on a river, you learn at an early age how to manage water that is constantly moving in one direction, wind or no wind. And if you capsize and find yourself in deep water you can drift out of it. (Through the years, I have saved the lives of at least two non-river people using this method.) But on a lake there are no currents and, more often than not, no bottom, and you are at the mercy of the wind, which is fickle as a deprived rooster and always a threat.

Looking back, I can now see the irresponsible things I have done; there were too many of us in one boat, and much of the time, we had left the shore without even the most untrustworthy of safety equipment. And of course, none of us were good swimmers, as river people never are. (Because river water is cold and fast moving and too shallow for swimming in by the time summer finally arrives and the temperatures warm.) I shiver at the thought of the disrespect I had for all waters.

Sometimes, I would put the boys in the boat and pole from our camp, a kilometre to the upper shore, where we all got out and waded from a gravel beach. The smaller two were instructed to stand in the more shallow areas. I can still see Jeff, the oldest, wearing my old chest waders, many times too big in the feet and so high on him that he had to turn them down and wrap a belt around his waist to keep them from slipping below his hips. He had to drag them along like a prisoner does his shackles. While Steven fished from the boat, which I had anchored out a ways, Jason wore my old hip boots that were also turned down, the straps wrapped around his thighs. If one of them had fallen into the water, he would have had absolutely no chance. It was as if I was sacrificing their safety in order to instruct them on the less important practices of angling.

Years ago, we angled that way, my sons and I. Over spirited springtime waters. And our love for the river, and each other, was like an old affair, or indeed an addiction that we had no desire to put away—those wonderful days when my boys were small and my mother and father were still well and active.

At birthday parties or special dinner celebrations, which were always held in the old farmhouse, after the meal and a sip of wine, we would sit around the dining-room table as the sun reflected through the window's lattice to make gold patterns on the cloth, and we'd tell lively stories of the day's events. Then, to please Daddy, we would hold hands while we sang in a hearty chorus "Shall We Gather at the River," his favourite air. I can still hear my sons' as well as my father's and mother's loud voices as they raised them in that old river hymn. The canoeists who passed our farm could have heard the singing.

My father used to tell us if we went to church on Sunday, we'd have better luck in the week that followed. If we couldn't get there for some good reason, God would understand. "But I wouldn't press my luck on that one if I were you, not least of all to hang out at the river."

And so we prayed, without witness, even as we fly-fished. For sure, the river was an addiction that was stronger than virtue, more holy than redemption.

Sometimes, too, in memory at least, my grandfather is there in song. And I can still hear the old man's shakey voice as he sat in the shadowy, lamp-lit parlour—which was wallpapered in patterns of big red flowers among strands of autumn grass—after a hard day's work in the fields or woods had made his bones ache, just as mine do now. And my grandmother rubbed his back and shoulders with Minard's White Liniment, which had been heated on the stove.

His once restless river spirit was by then weakening, so that he would drop off to sleep sitting upright, pale and gaunt as a phantom, realizing finally that his best days were behind him. And when he awoke, he sang, yes he sang, loud and clear, not one of our songs certainly, but rather an old air from his boyhood. And in the words of this song I saw images of Papa's own father, with the long flowing beard and his shoulders sloped—from a lifetime of carrying railway ties to the sailing ships—as he made his way from the spring with a pail of water in each hand.

I'm rolling home to merry England,
Rolling home across the sea.

And he would play this tune and others on his little asthmatic accordion.

Sometimes Papa sang with his son-in-law Hugh Campbell, a tall man with a high-pitched voice who had come home from the First World War with two steel rifle bullets in his back. (These were too close to the spine to be removed surgically without fear of paralyzing Uncle Hughie, so he lived in pain from 1917 until his death in the fall of 1952.) These men sang while my grandmother carried drinks to them. Sometimes they sang all night, their heads lifting in the chorus like hens drinking. And the lamp grew low in oil so that its chimney smoked like a stove pipe and left a brown ring on the whitewashed ceiling, while polluting the air with the stench of a charred wick. This singing would not have been for entertainment, rather for the memories that such tunes carried in their melodies and lyrics. Those old songs would have been passed down from generation to generation—without being recorded electronically—and I suspect this gave those men nostalgic images of their youth, of posterity, of family values, and a feeling of peace within themselves. It was a kind of game they played to see who remembered more of them or if anyone remembered all of one song, which quite often had twenty-odd verses.

That was Papa's father. That was Papa. That was Hugh Campbell. That was my father and mother. That was my sons and me. That is my grandsons. Yes, it gave us all a sense of contentment and belonging. I suppose that was why we all sang. That is why we sing today.

Life was like that until my sons had grown into big lads and insisted on going in their own directions and at their own times, as if it were embarrassing for them as maturing adults to be seen following along in the old ways with their kinfolk. Or to even join in the singing. Along the way, they had outgrown me and my parents and had developed their own ideas about rivers and equipment and fly presentations and safety and a hundred other things about life on the river and elsewhere that I or my folks did not know. And of course their music was outlandish. They had become more sophisticated in their ways than the older family members ever could be.

And for some reason, I felt they had grown away from the family values. It became a struggle to get them to show up at the traditional May picnic, to stand, tackle in hand—with the river in the background—for a photograph with the larger family circle, to come together for a canoe run. I guess there just isn't much time for such trivial things in a busy modern life. I supposed that as they went through high school and college, they started to follow the new fads they had been reading about in the more far-reaching books, as well as in the international magazines they had subscribed to, the television programs and the Internet, all of which made easy access to information that had passed the rest of us by years, if not decades, before. And this was not only about the river, but life in general.

Now I can see these new approaches being practised when Jeff and Lori take my grandsons, Samuel and Joshua, to the river.

I get excited every time I watch the grandchildren getting rigged up to go fishing with their parents. And this is more important to me than anything that can happen to them in the way of catching a fish. I always rest easier when I see the boys are being fitted with the best life jackets of the day and other up-to-date safety equipment, and that before the boat leaves the shore they are sitting still, while their father moves the craft forward. Sometimes I can hear their soft voices as they join in a song.

And it makes me proud when I watch from my chair on the veranda, as the little ones receive their instructions, not only on safety and technique, but also on the value of the river, the conservation of the resource, and the appreciation of the scenery, the birds, and the fresh air. I am amused when bits and pieces of the old equipment and some old advice have been handed down, yet again. And I wonder where my grandsons will go to university, what will become of them, and if there will be an end to the ever-changing times.

I feel good about having planted a seed, for having taken my sons as a family unit to experience the rivers and woods so long ago. And for having taught them to do not what I did, exactly, but what I said—until they could move on to something better—as my father and mother had done for me, a long time before. And for keeping the music in life because it is medicine for the soul.

I can see myself in my sons and even the grandsons. And when I look into a mirror, more and more now, I see my father and grandfather in myself, and I feel a responsibility to uphold that old river legacy.

Maybe I have done something right after all.

River Voices

I can hear them from the bed in my cabin, summer nights, when it appears as though their calls will never end. And each one carries in it an image, a fleeting moment from somewhere in the past, in the same way that a smell, the taste of a certain berry, or the sounds of a distant church bell might take one to a romantic time and place.

These river voices I'm speaking of, they come from the osprey, the eagle, and the loon. And there is the two-fold splash of leaping salmon—which leaves widening rings that sparkle in the moonlight, and a different sound from that of the kingfisher or the beaver—as they head upstream after fighting the fast water in the bend below home. There is shrillness in the voices expelled by the millions of insects that inhabit the cedar swamp in back of the camp; and I now find a measure of contentment in the thin, ringing sounds offered up by the lowly toad whose June voice carries for kilometres on the water. Or even in something as subtle as the cow's breath of south wind that whispers through the backdoor screens and pushes its river fragrance into the poorly ventilated, bat-smelling camp.

The distant rumble of thunder energizes my nightmares and makes me sit up in a half-sleep to stare at the log walls as though they are a fortress, built from heavy timbers long ago by my father and me, to protect me from just such cannon fire. I contemplate where in the woods each has grown, while lightning fills the zenith with reflections and breathes fresh air into the oppressive, sultry night. This midnight storm is followed by the rain-cleansed winds, very real sunrises, smells, and flavours that carry me from high spring to summer, to autumn and, metaphorically, into winter. Each season here brings all the promise of a new beginning, as if I were a newcomer to the river, but with a duffle bag of old habits, old relations.

A gentle breeze touches the white pine to make its boughs toss and sigh and brush my board roof, reminding me that I had planted that tree, decades ago, in memory of you. And now you are pitching memory against reality (the innocence and passions of our first love), to console me, dissuade me from my thoughts, deepen my sleep. And there is the sprinkling of pine needles, the old tent rains that carry in them the pleasurable voices of childhood, back when time did not exist. And dreams were more real than memory.

They take me to a night when I slept out of doors with my older brother and was frightened by an owl. We had pitched our new tent in the dooryard, had gotten under the covers at dark and gone to sleep. But sometime in the night, I awoke, short of breath, because the dampness from the cold ground had stirred up my asthma. And I was nervous in the dark when my brother would not wake up. It was then the "whoo-whoos" from a barn owl made me panic. I scampered into the house and to my bedroom, which was upstairs over the kitchen. My brother followed, complaining that I had spoiled our sleep-out. I would never stay in a tent again.

Sometimes, on hollow summer nights, I am kept awake by the chuckle of McKenzie Brook as it trickles into the river just across from my cabin. McKenzie Brook, and the howl of tires on the chip-seal highway as party people find their way home from the social clubs. A fly buzzes in the lighted bathroom, and the old clock that stands on my night table, a constant reminder of the impasse of time, offers a piteous "Tick, tock, Tick, tock"; its glow-in-the-dark hands are frozen at half-past two or three. When I am awake at this hour it seems like nothing tangible exists, nothing except this small cubicle with its sloppy book shelves and their whispering night characters. These storied people are not diversions, rather symbols that help activate my old delights, which to me are as near to God as I can get, but whose strongest qualities always evaporate before morning. I know, too, that the human spirit can easily spin out of control at this insomniac time of night and that a sleeping pill is inevitable. Still, for me, real happiness is not possible without solitude, frayed or otherwise, and this kind of spiritual turbulence, I believe, breeds originality.

At the break of day I hear "O-oh sweet Canada, Canada, Canada" from the white-throated sparrow, which has its nest over the river, in a bottomland I refer to as the Elm Tree Meadow. This is a sweet river sound, heard even before the ovenbird or the dove has awakened to start its morning coos.

And there are moose birds, for which I have built feeding trays, because their presence restores an easiness of mind, a refreshing kind of escapism, like the whiskey jack brought me so long ago, in the old school grounds when I broke away from the class to eat my bread-and-jam sandwich at half-past eleven. Those sacred birds ate from my palms. They are now symbols of life and death. Papa always described them as the spirits of our deceased woods and river people. My parents and grandparents are among them. And some classmates, too.

On summer days, from the camp yard, I can hear the high-pitched voices of the tube rafters who drift past, so many in a row that for a time the river appears like a doughnut factory. This annoys the sport fishers who Spey cast in the salmon waters just downstream from the cabin. And I can hear their shouts. All are river people for a day, a week, a month, or even a season, and then they move on to new places, new things.

But the natural river sounds are voices more than living things, a quality prose, that for me determines the spirit of this river as an ecology. And this activity invigorates the murmur of so many ancestral ghosts. They appear in the early morning fog like artifacts, experiences from the past, which rise off the froth-dappled water to dance awhile and turn the rising sun into a crimson beach ball. They whisper in my good ear above the gentle tossing of the waves or the jingle of the wind chimes from out on the veranda. I have linked each of them to some feeling. The passion of my first love lingers in water that trickles under a morning bridge, where the stars had reflected upon washed gravel as we kissed. Or the morning winds that whisper along the eavestroughing and carry the sounds of April, a time when the family had concern about father's safety as he worked on a spring-high river, knowing that he could not swim a stroke.

These voices, or at least the images that accompany them, have been unconsciously placed years ago among my memory's archives to be revived on nights like this. They were spawned, if the truth were told, from a childhood that was carefree, reckless, even romantic, like an old James Dean movie. Yes, it was a countrified upbringing, one removed from the cultivation and stimulation found in city places, the more refined voices of academia, the arts and culture, classical music, dance and literature, or the inspiration and perhaps even the creativity I could have discovered in the lecture halls of the university professor and other disciplined, philosophic people. The speaking soul of the river was to me, as a child of the earth, my principal teacher.

That life could be realized in the confines of books was never really within my way of thinking. And the idea that words, instead of symbols, could be used to convey my true feelings in life as in art, that these river sounds could be lifted from out of the half-darkness and made into literature was a kind of paradox. For my river voices appeared to convey the feelings opposite to those of the written word and were on opposing ends of what was being taught in the classroom. Maybe this perception came from the discipline that prevailed therein, a lack of freedom that gave new meaning to words without sounds, a diction that carried no earthy symbols. As a youth I did not know about or understand such scholarly enunciations.

Or indeed, miss them. Instead, I found stimulation and motivation in the sounds of the earth and the voices of the river.

You see, unlike the privileged city youth, this river child had been raised in the outlands, had quit grade school to help my grandfather run the farm when my father was wounded in a hunting accident the fall that I was thirteen. While I felt that giving up school to help the family was a noble cause, and I had become the hero of my younger siblings for the time that Daddy was laid up—I loved the sense of importance with which they treated me—I would have to say, at the time, I was travelling in a regressive direction, that I had been influenced (perhaps subconsciously) by my grandfather and his century-old ways. For that was the course he had taken, and because I admired and loved him, I wanted to follow just then.

It was as if I was afraid to embrace the best minds of my place and time, follow my own instincts, while seeing my life's secret ambitions being depleted in me, the desire to go after my long-range goals, which I suppose, if I had been more able to think for myself, would have included a classroom education and mythologies that reached beyond the river. Rather, I was content with a short-sighted, old-home view, which by then was already being exhausted into a comfortable circumstance, the lives we were forced to live, or thought we were forced to live. It was just so much easier to stay at home and not pursue anything beyond what was an immediate concern to me and my family.

It was as if I didn't want to look too far down the road, gamble away what I felt I could not afford to lose, put strain on a fragile confidence that was already being eroded. And after my father's accident, I was afraid of what could happen to my family, left in the hands of my grandfather who was so old by then he had to urinate sitting down. Who would put the bread and beans on the supper table? Who would pay the doctor bills? Who would do the house repairs? I could see our farm being overtaken by governments for back taxes or our shores sold off to foreigners for a little money to help us survive the winter, scary thoughts for a vulnerable youngster, but nevertheless threats that were very real. For there were no social programs in those days, and when something happened to the breadwinner, the older sons were expected to take charge.

So I rolled up my sleeves, became a man without actually experiencing a childhood, even though my father was by then on the quick road to recovery. (He had been laid up for only a few months.) I just would not take my mother's advice and go back to school, become a child again, having already considered myself "grown up." I could not try to fit into the younger, yet more scholarly way of life, which I knew would be a struggle and an embarrassment after being away from the classroom for almost two years. I would have had to give up my own sense of importance. For I hated books by this time and saw them only as an obstacle that obstructed my view, something for children to ponder. And of course, Mum and the teacher were the only ones fighting to have me do this. My father and grandfather were pleased that I had been so noble as to quit school and join the workforce.

In truth, I had used my father's accident as an excuse to quit school because the classroom was taking me away from the outdoor life I so loved. Yes, it was depriving me from being the man on horseback with a Winchester rifle in his saddle scabbard, a revolver at his hip like the red-blooded heroes I had been watching at the movie house, hearing on the radio, or reading about in the ten-cent comic books I bought in the village.

And there were those rowdy, local mentors I had already taken up with in real life. These were the school dropouts who hitchhiked to the village for a pack of cigarettes, a haircut, and a new shirt with the snap-down pocket flaps. They went to the dances on Saturday nights, drank rum, and fought one another. Not a great influence, I can see now.

As a consequence, nature became my best teacher, and experience alone was the only preventative when it came to avoiding calamity. I was being guided by the delusions of nature, T.S. Eliot's "brown fog" of the wilderness. The only things I showed any real dedication to—because I knew nothing else—were the axe and power saw, the rod and gun, tools to be used in my sweat-of-the-brow labour and the gathering of wild game and fish, as I had vowed to be the breadwinner. Thus became my involvement with the workforce, too young, and the predatory habits I now believe to be among the shortfalls that followed any rebel dropout through life. It was a state of mind I carried inside me until I was a grown man, believing the practical lifestyle I had pursued—at that early age—was the right one, and that I would not be proven wrong by anyone who had come along a road less rocky than the one I had travelled.

As for culture, I had learned at a young age to appreciate the folk ballads sung by men like my grandfather and father in their mackinaw coats, the strains of a cheap country fiddle—I played one at house parties and dance halls and was applauded by the older people for it—and the whoops and heavy-footed clods of the local woodsmen and truck drivers after a little nip. These and the cowboy-hat-and-gun opera that played on Saturday nights at the old movie house in Blackville. Around home, as well, there was a long-established tradition that was very much entrenched in religion, myths, forerunners, ghosts, guardian angels, omens, and long-running superstitious habits—things that city people referred to as "rural gothic." And each of these had its own desperate voice, its own fears, its own consequences. Those voices haunt me even now.

Sometimes, here at my river camp in the early mornings, I can hear the muffled engines of all-terrain vehicles. They sound like the drumming of partridge wings. And there are the mumbling sounds, the haw-haws of local anglers, my age and older, who come to wade into the salmon pool below home and cast their flylines. As of old, their moving lines create miniature rainbows against that silvery mist as the morning sun touches them. (You can tell an angler's personality by the gracefulness with which they cast a flyline.) Their voices blend with the sounds of the water, their clothes unify with the landscape, as they take their turn in the pool when a fish rises. And then they return to sit in a shanty by a makeshift stove that burns shore grass or cow dung to ward off the mosquitoes. Their smoke makes a cocoon over the flats as the men and women reminisce, old people's weaknesses perhaps, but I believe it is more about coming to terms with their own ghosts.

Because these local anglers are survivors and have lived comfortable and healthy lives so close to the land—without chasing after big money or lofty academic endeavours—theirs is a conversation that is filled with real-life experiences. And I know first-hand that for them it has been a rustic life, one in which the heartfelt beliefs have been spoken without the influence of books, passions that have expressed their most elementary feelings, and where the elaborate phrase was never substituted for the natural image. For sure, they communicated their loves of the river, of nature, and each other, more openly because they have been, in the words of Wordsworth, "less under the influence of social vanity." And a beautiful love is allowed to happen without its participants analyzing one another to death because they follow their hearts and not some form of social blueprint. There is the sweetening of a past that is influenced by nostalgia, of dreams and wishes, still alive, after so many years, a bucket list of past attempts still to be reactivated, and some lesser hopes that are yet to be energized into dream status. All without the help of rule books or the university lecturer. As of old, they are here looking for a fish for the dinner table. For them, fly-fishing is not a taboo to be frowned upon by the environmentalist or the city slicker, not a fad, not an addiction, not a newcomer's obsession; it's a traditional way of life, like the gathering of firewood, the picking of berries, or the digging of potatoes. And for a brief moment I am there among them, shaking the warm hands of the past, sharing in the stoking of the grass fire, the puffing of the bellows, feeling the eye-sting of smoke, the bending rod, the line that comes to life and nourishes one's body and soul with a sense of accomplishment (and the anticipation of potential praise from elders), when a fish touches it and gets hooked. Even after so many years, the sounds of a leaping salmon, the singing of a fly reel combined with a spring wind that whispers through the trees still remain expressions of hope, desire, and of conscience, dream noises from a world of good times.

And the protective voice is still alive; the angry defiance of the river's native sons and daughters as they stand up for the wilderness as it used to be, the old order of things that could or would not change, not for them. And I guess, not for me. These people speak to me of culture more than anything I have ever found in books. Their voices reverberate in the back of my mind, not like the ambiguous lessons I got later from the lecture halls, but from the early life and the river experiences themselves.

For it was in those young times, those young places that I now believe I observed more, thought more clearly, because it was about real life, heartfelt emotions as I had experienced them and not ones I had read about in books. It was not a portrayal of what real life should have been as seen through the eyes of someone else, perhaps with less true-life experience than I had myself, or God forbid, someone I was trying to impress. For only the true river sounds were original, anything institutional or copied we looked upon as a form of plagiarism.

For me now, this place has gone back to being a voice more than a river, more than a time of day, a time of night, a time of life. More than a youthful adventure, more than a senior citizen with insomnia, trying to get a decent night's sleep—after a shot of whiskey—so near to nature. It's the voice of old home and family, and yes, it's still an escape to find my true self. This voice, though I am hard of hearing, gets louder as I grow older. It returns to nourish me like a parent whose memories have withstood time and which I revisit for comfort and the healing powers they possess, and like the schoolteacher who always had my best interest at heart, even though I didn't believe it at the time. (Teachers were always voices. And the greater the teacher, the more powerful the voice.)

When I was a schoolboy I never questioned the profoundness, never doubted the sincerity of the classroom; I just escaped to the river to think things through. It was a trial and error process and one by which I was trying to find my own true consciousness, my own expression. I could always do this at the river. And even now on nights like this, when I am half-oblivious, when I know I'm not really asleep, yet I'm dreaming, the old river speaks to me as though I am her self-seeking favourite son. And I feel good about just being here, and I ponder the idea of building another room on the cabin.

For me, the river is still a place to recalibrate when life is going off the rails, like returning to an old and easy study. And because I am an island of sorts (an anarchist by some people's standards), my findings are not meant to coincide with those of others; no one else can possibly know the dreams and memories that are spawned from them. I suppose they are somewhere between the two schools of thought, the two streams of consciousness—the self-taught man versus the institutionally educated one. But with a greater accent towards the old river itself, its teaching and healing powers.

These are the voices that appear in the night. They are in dream sequences, and so they are recurring.

Voices can be heard for a long way on the water at this time of the night, this time of life, especially if the air is humid and there is no wind. They are like the voices we hear from inside a rain barrel, images more than word phrases, but nonetheless a part of the common river sounds which we, the rural people, have become accustomed to hearing. For me they inspire precious moments, all of which unravel in the night like a distorted and jerky black-and-white film from the old movie house.

I am trying to tell you these things and am making a poor attempt at it, because no word description of memory or dream or premonition can convey the true sensation, the actuality that shapes itself without the use of human lips, and which as time passes, is glorified with the brush stroke of nostalgia. In the words of Marlow from *The Heart of Darkness* by Joseph Conrad, a man who never grew away from his river, "We live, as we dream—alone."

It matters to no one else.

The River Influence

In my search for individualism and what path I should follow through life, I had a schoolboy's belief that the mind could never be nourished wholly by books, rather by life itself—actions that came out of ideas, that came out of feelings—and that the spirit is always master of the flesh. I felt that one should follow one's dream when it came to achieving self-satisfaction and to leaving a legacy. This made me think that "book people," or those I had perceived to have been "intellectuals," belonged in easier and more civilized places than the one where I was growing up; they would not fit into my world, not easily. And of course I knew that I could never fit into theirs.

When it came to voices, when it came to lessons learned, this river child would hear only what was real, literally. I would experience what my heart and senses wanted me to, as I followed my own instincts through life with my feet planted firmly on the ground. As far as I could see, there were no earth-shattering symbols, no longevity, or heartfelt memories that could come from the words of books. Not like the lessons entrenched by seeing the good and ill of human nature first-hand, the emotions felt after each telling wilderness experience.

Certainly, my early life was far removed from the printed page, from academic institutions, and the rules of art and science. Rather it was rooted deep in the country and on the river. In 1955, when I was twelve years old, I wrote to the National Sports Council in New York City and received the Manly Art of Self Defence Home Course, boxing lessons offered by ex-champion Joe Louis. And ten-ounce gloves, from Eaton's of Canada mail-order catalogue. These things, according to my father and grandfather, would make a man out of me. At the time, the university degree, as far as I could understand it, was there only for the "privileged" youth, city people who were deprived of real-life experiences (except perhaps through a stint at summer camp), and so not genuine in the rural sense of the word. They were people who had no field experience and absolutely no practical skills when it came to surviving in the out-of-doors. They had no coping powers when it came to dealing with hardship and trauma. And of course, the least little dilemma became an "issue" that was unmanageable.

Summer holidays should never be compared to real life in the country. Nor should the short-lived back-to-land movements of the would-be farmers who come, now and then, toting their fiddles and banjos, perhaps going organic for a season or two, experiencing but a few country hardships, before heading back to the city with a new verse to sing. Or the vegetarian cousins who came from the city for a summer, only to find that they were allergic to cut grass, ragweed, and pollen. It is all different when you are here for the long haul. You live and grow with the miseries, sensing the things you should avoid, while developing an immune system that will help you cope.

As a youth, up early each morning, I headed to the woods where I worked the long days, sometimes in snow up to my waist. With energy to burn and fuelled by an underdog's ambition, the old man's praise, and that rural dogma I've been trying to describe, I earned money enough to buy myself new boots, GWG blue jeans, and a western shirt, which I wore to the village (as far away as I wanted to go and, indeed, into a different world) on Saturday nights. There was no life beyond these times and places.

Back then, I felt that for a person to live and to die in the city, God forbid, and to spend their entire lifetime in books was not to have experienced real life at all. (I was not a reader back then.) This was what I had been told by my fellow country people; and I believed it to be true. At that time—I was approaching my teens—I had never been to a big city, nor did I want to be there. Not for a minute. So that culture had no place in my dream world.

You see, to the deep-rooted country folk, urban people were always looked upon as transient souls, people who were somewhat less than whole, who would spend their years looking for a place to take root. And not find it. As Leo Tolstoy's Pozdnyshev in *The Kreutzer Sonata* put it, "In town a man can live a hundred years without noticing that he has long been dead and has rotted away. He has no time to take account of himself, he is always occupied."

As far as I was concerned, country life was the bee that had a song to sing, the physically active participant when it came to the workings of the hive.

City people were folks who I felt would walk through time like opera house phantoms, with no sense of love or nostalgia toward the land, or for that matter their fellow city dwellers who would nod to a homeless person on the street and walk on by. For the aged, especially the ones who spent a lifetime chasing after the dollar and were deprived of it for reasons beyond their control—illness, politics, or just bad luck—for them there would be, as Robert Frost put it in "The Death of the Hired Man," "nothing to look backward to with pride, / And nothing to look forward to with hope," no old home to which, "when you have to go there, / They have to take you in." The keeper of the old would have to be an institution, at best.

But in the country, the home, with its real-life experiences and its traditions, was supreme because it meant security, even in old age. Especially in old age. To us, the townspeople were different from not only country people, but the birds, animals, and fish as well, all of which were homing creatures. This growing of traditions, this turbulent but good life as I knew it then, this security, even though it was said by townspeople to have harboured a bit of cultural poverty, took many, many generations to establish.

However, I knew as well, I always knew that in the country the relationship between art and life itself was kept at arm's length, if not hidden or even forbidden. And those of us who were a bit more sensitive, who thought art had a connection with real life and that both were unique in their strong character, paid for it. We were made fun of as being a mouse in a man's world, being "tender-hearted." And we fought this, too. Yes, we fought our own sensitivities because we felt they were unacceptable, even embarrassing to reveal, while you could say that the opposite was true.

We all spoke in a macho country lingo that we could not hear and which would take years to grow out of. And if we didn't speak in the local slang, we were mocked. As Wallace Stegner wrote in *Wolf Willow*, "You grow up speaking one dialect and reading and writing another."

But, as I found out later, this was the case in suburbia as well, although theirs was a more fashionable jargon, and because of their numbers, more widely accepted. (This is no longer true in either place, as both worlds are now influenced by the age of information. And most kids from my son's generation are college educated.) It never occurred to me until many years later that what we felt back then was unique and original and could be put to good use in our writings and other forms of art. For it was something to cling to, the good life: no smog, not that we could see, not in our Eden; no criminal intent that we were not aware of, or that we could not swing in a positive direction. What was a criminal but someone with good intentions who had perhaps been abused early on and had gone sour on life?

Only later, when I realized there was more to life than watching the grass grow after an April rain or killing potato bugs by sprinkling them with a powdery, pink poison while the morning dew was still on the leaves, did I take to the books. Or when, in the words of William Wordsworth's "Ode: Intimations of Immortality," "Shades of the prison-house begin to close / Upon the growing boy." I became a reader when I discovered that something strange was happening inside me, something that had come about in an ever so subtle way. Was it a green shoot perhaps? Was it a bug? I had heard somewhere that it is the beginning of wisdom when you recognize that the best you can do is to choose which rules you want to live by. And that vocation is the legitimate child of necessity as well as inner happiness. But where could I find an education except through the institution?

I went back to school at the age of twenty-six. For the next fourteen years I attended night school university classes where I studied literature—from Geoffrey Chaucer to T.S. Eliot—while holding down a full-time job. And I hate to think where I would be today without that experience.

By that time in my life, everything came doubly hard for me; everything I read was contradictory to the old home whimsy and superstitions, the established wisdom of the land and river people. In a sense I was a misguided man clinging to a boy's world. Yes, I set out to market late, as so many in the country had done, to seek the satisfaction I was craving (but could not exactly comprehend), and certainly could not find around "home," to become a different person, one wherein my head would overrule my heart. And the distance between my melancholy past and the present, or so I felt, would grow into separate worlds more quickly than I ever would have thought possible.

I did not realize then that country life, its way of dealing with things through participation and the experiences passed down—the traditions that repeated themselves and repeated themselves, many of which followed the seasons of the year and the seasons of life—was something that one does not grow out of in one generation or even two or three; it's all so deep-rooted.

But I knew that if I had a stronghold it was my sensitivities.

To paraphrase a notion from Marcel Proust's *In Search of Lost Time,* I realized then that it could have been only through the arts that I could emerge from myself. By that time I wanted to shake free of that little person I could see myself becoming if I stayed in that old groove, like the people around me, many of whom talked with one voice, saw things from one slant, heard only what they wanted to hear; folks with whom I was by then becoming bored.

Even as I did so, even as I struggled to find my place, to knock down doors in the intellectual world—like Thomas Hardy's Jude at Christminster—even while I had a craving to learn, it was a struggle to discipline myself to shake free of the old mindset. I had to take on a completely new way of thinking. And as I did so, I felt a betrayal toward the land and river, toward the things I had been so close to in nature, the beauty and bliss as seen through those youthful eyes, the innocence, the healing powers, the heartfelt oversoul that a wilderness home can provide a person who doubts his ability to face the outside world and the structured institutional life.

And I wondered, how does one know where true happiness lies? How does one know what inspires creativity and originality?

Which path should one follow through such a yellow wood? Schools teach us to support their own philosophies and agendas and are not altogether free-thinking either. And do the universities have an agenda of their own? Does the lecture hall offer up a different slant on life? Or is it a brainwashing of a certain ideology? Does someone with a good mind need the institution? Or are we better left to self-educate? (Robert Frost, a man who dropped out of university, claimed that he could listen to someone speak for two minutes and tell you what school that person had attended.) While I believed that some formal education was necessary, I still figured that artistic intellectualism, the sensitivities of feeling and seeing things from a new and more personal slant was the greater vice. Because it was original. And in the arts, uniqueness accounts for everything. You have to have the distinct voice to succeed. And the former, the persuasions of the lecture hall, should not interfere or corrupt the latter when it comes to the pursuit of art in any form. Neither the rules of academe nor the influence should enter into the artistic expression or the quest for individualism. And to this end, the self-taught man, the one with less institutional baggage, had the advantage when it came to creating new artistic genius. For it is said that the best wine comes out of the worst possible growing conditions.

So I questioned, which voices should we listen to as we grow into adulthood and beyond? Or should we just follow our hearts, our own personal gods. Our time is short and once we set out on a given path through the wilderness, it is not that easy to swing life in another direction. Time, our only real measuring stick, moves so quickly toward that autumnal regression, mental decay that comes with the years. And I have always believed we have a habit of abandoning, too young, what we love most, the environment, the subtleties of nature, the innocence, the originality, the conscientiousness with which the old country home and family had been founded; we give it all up for some form of institutional gamble, a mainstream way of thinking that erodes our uniqueness. And so I hungered, perhaps unconsciously, for the new start. As I crave for it now, even though I have spent a lifetime in books. (For words can never truly convey an author's most heartfelt beliefs or the in-depth reaction from a telling experience.) Because there is no beginning or ending to things such as the growth of the mind, no real way in which to measure genius, no starting point, no finish line. And by this time, I am aware that satisfaction slips away as soon as you realize you have it and say to yourself that you are totally happy with your success and you cannot do more.

Until early adulthood, I had learned to suppress my desire for any kind of inner growth, to ignore the subtleties—the strongest heart feelings—because I was told that to feel too deeply was to be effeminate. I had been trained to think small, and this had left me with few options. In the way of all country children of that place and age, my morality was already being determined by obligation and responsibility. There was no time or preparation for a successful life beyond the line fences of the farm. And God forbid, not in the arts. In those early years, even if there had been time, I could not have imagined myself going to work in the office of an art gallery or working toward being a teacher in some distant school or university. Such a lifestyle was beyond reach, even in my dreams. And not macho. Neither would these people want someone of a rural background in their midst, even as a board member. Especially as a social-climbing board member.

Now, I wonder how I might have responded to the opportunity had it arisen from out of a different past, or how I would have grown from that vantage point. I shiver to think of it. For I cannot imagine myself sitting at the boardroom tables of an art gallery and playing the politics that surround such places, with the goal of someday becoming chair of the board or perhaps even some kind of head curator with no brush stroke of his or her own. (While like the librarian, the curator—as keeper of the art—has a noble profession, it would not be my station in life.) Or to walk from classroom to classroom with a lecture on the works of Hemingway or Faulkner, men who had been raised in the country, were free-thinking spirits, and had their own unique styles so far removed from what was being taught in writing classes. Yet, they have each won the Nobel Prize for literature.

These literary awards were not given for following the herd; rather, they were accolades of gratitude for the unique voice. These men drew from their real-life experiences. (I know this because when I read their biographies I ran into the same "fictional" characters.)

And I wonder, I often wonder, if someone who had not grown up in the country of my boyhood would even hear or recognize the voices I am describing. Or if these urban people have other aspirations to nurture, other demons inside their little circles with which to wrestle. Or if there was ever a need for them to escape their environment—as I had a desire to escape my own—to the cottage perhaps, without a book, where they could witness nature first-hand, grasp an internal heartstring to see in what direction it took them ? For sure, I would not be able to relate to the urban voices of another's childhood, that youthful city environment. Nor could I connect with the cement jungle, the frantic workings of the human beehive, the intellectual jackhammer, the politics, and always with sweaty palms.

You see, to the long-standing country dweller, the city resident (even with degrees on a sleeve) is far removed from the rural mindset that makes a place real, the landscape out of which some of the best poets and philosophers are conceived, thinkers like William Butler Yeats of Howth, William Wordsworth of the Lake District, Margaret Laurence of Neepawa, William Faulkner of New Albany, and Robert Frost of Ripton.

And I still believe that great things can happen here among my people, too. This must happen here. This has happened here: it has happened already from the influences of writers like Max Aitken, David Adams Richards, and Alden Nowlan (all of whom were school dropouts and largely self-taught), people who give us a sense of rural ownership, a feeling that we really belong to this place and time, that this river is our home, we are its proud citizenry, and we do not have to take a back seat to anyone just because they come from somewhere else or have attended a certain school. We are a proud river people.

For in the end, the development of great minds has nothing to do with where they come from or whether they are self-educated or classroom taught. It has more to do with where they are heading. And with how much desire and free will they go forward. If the ambition is there, along with a desire for innovation, the cream will come to the surface and the greater voices will be heard. I guarantee. And if there is no great desire to succeed, schooling itself will take us nowhere.

Alden Nowlan said that he had quit school in grade three. "That was a mistake," he told me. "If I had it to do over again, I would not have gone at all."

But there is a crust of long-established city people (the cream of society), who believe that a person should be measured not by their great ideas, individual ambitions, and motivations, or even originality, rather by what they bring with them in the way of posterity, lineage, degrees, political connections, and their dollar values. Wealth and titles are held in more esteem than talent. For me there is a great sadness that accompanies this concept because so many young minds have taken advantage of being trained (if not educated) within our finest schools.

Originality and greatness come from within us. We get inspiration from our dreams, and in the end we are the architects of our own legacy.

Autumnal River

Here on the river the seasons change from summer to autumn overnight. At the first scream of a Canada jay or the staccato cackle of a cock-of-the-woods, the hot and balmy days of August are replaced with a brooding sky, sullen winds, and driving rain. These carry in them the ghosts of October, the scent of burning potato stalks, the orange glow of a pumpkin sitting on our veranda steps. It is a subtle foretelling, not easily described, and is first noticed in the cool morning air before the sun has risen high enough to shorten the shadows of riverside trees. And the tiny patches of foam that drift down on the water do not evaporate until almost noon, when the warmth comes back into the land—ever so slowly—in places the sunshine touches.

We feel it again in the evenings, when the coppery sunsets are followed by an even more brassy moon that rises over the tree-topped horizon, and all of a sudden the dampness is penetrating our summer clothes. These changes in the season are not talked about, rather observed with a sense of foreboding, and there is a secret bonding among us because we know, down deep, that we have already slipped into another autumn. And we set out to search for our wool sweaters and home-knit gloves.

On a September evening, everything in the northeast turns to charcoals and blacks, and a chill falls over the land, making our wind-sheltered campsite, which was so cheerful in the sunlit afternoon, to be in Papa's words, "As cold and desolate as a sheepfold." During the lengthening autumn nights, we observe as the temperatures drop to well below freezing and a hoarfrost whitens the fields so that the dying grass looks like an old man's hair, bent and twisted and quite uncombed. But the air is fresh and clear at this season, and a church bell, so remote, can be heard along the water for many kilometres.

It is my favourite time of the year to be on the river or in the woods.

A few warm days can bring back the summer temporarily, so that migrating robins may pause to rest awhile from their long flights south; their clear, redundant chirp is reminiscent of spring and summer, which have already become lost seasons because they are too close behind us to be recorded romantically in our gilded memories. Still, as we pause for a moment to reflect, we grieve for the canoe trip we did not take, the aged relative we didn't visit, or the grand barbecue to which all the people we love or admire were to be invited but we did not have time to host.

Where has the summer gone?

Our tans are fading beneath long-sleeved jackets, but out of habit, after hearing the robin and feeling the kiss of sunshine, we go back to wearing our summer clothes for an hour or even an afternoon. We walk in the fields of after-growth and try to follow the flight of the now songless grasshopper or the bumblebee in its listless journey through the frostbitten bramble. It is as if the bee is also trying to appear cheerful, as it offers up an abbreviated version of its old hum, audible in small pockets between the gusts of wind that sweep over our potato lands, where corrugated furrows lie open like the pages of a Bible. And the free-spirited chickadee, as if out of an obligation, performs its artistic little song before moving on to wherever the wind blows it.

Through the recent afternoons, we have watched as our summer birds flocked in the fields of amber stubble. They assembled to roost on power lines like notes on sheet music, scores so blessed they are held up by cedar crosses. And in the Elm Tree Meadow, the wildflowers have already faded, even as they've ripened toward their autumnal hues. As the sun recedes into that downriver horizon, the water goes from blue to gold to silver, to a bed of spooling tar.

Our salmon have also blended in with the orange and the brown leaves, with here and there a speck of red, like the berries on an ivied veranda. The aggressive nature of these fish, their fighting spirit and frantic desire to reproduce at this time of the year, helps to accentuate the tough and robust character of this river and its people. After we've had supper in our big farmhouse kitchens, and when our evening chores are finally done, it is our second nature to hurry to the shore. My brother Gary and I pole our father's old board boat to centre stream and drop its oblong rock anchor, which is fixed to a mooring chain that extends from the boat's bow. And the hollow evening sounds of the water pulling the iron links over the gunwale resemble the firing of a Gatling gun. This spooks and angers the fish for a time so that they jump and scoot around us, making deep swells on the surface. We stand in our bare feet in the boat's stale and sun-warmed water, and we fish, one on each side, casting in rotation, each one watching for a salmon to splash at his hook.

We angle and listen to the shrill, glad voices of the children as they play their little summer games, one more time. They have missed the best hours of this day, shut up in a classroom, and now they run with vigour to take advantage of what daylight remains, to cram a day's gaming into a few precious minutes. As if in their confinement through this sunny afternoon, the thought of the past and now seemingly eventless summer has been brought vividly to their minds also, and with a touch of regret for not having done enough out of doors.

They play hard and loud, as if they also want to make the most of the bare, stubbled meadows before the coming of autumn rains and then the snow. And in their excited voices our own childhood comes back to us, and for a brief moment, we share in their small country pleasures, for we, too, feel that we have been tricked by the seasons.

The elderly predict that this will be "a long open fall, because the new moon is in the south and sitting upright like the sole of a rocking horse."

But we have heard all this before and know that each season speaks for itself; the melancholy downriver sunsets say it all.

We listen to the honking of Canada geese, those beautiful birds that fly in wavering Vs up the river, southwest out of the country. And we smell the children's leaf fires, glimpse the clouds of white and brown smoke drifting with a forlorn air over the water like an incense that harbours our ancestral ghosts. These traditional bonfires light up the autumn fields, while scattering the seeds of life and afterlife, keeping alive the genes and the customs of all those we love, who are now gone from this land and water. Our memories of them mingle in our souls, becoming part of our imaginations: the legend, the myth.

For you see, ours is a mythical river.

Tonight the old home pool is smooth and free-flowing as it trickles over the brown stones in the evening sunlight. As it has been doing for a zillion years. The water is clear as glass and cold as iced ammonia because it is spring-fed just now. The underwater grass has ripened and broken loose on the rise, drifting down and clinging to exposed rocks like slime that gathers at the edges of a rain barrel. Snipes flit from rock to rock, insect to insect. Beyond the pool, out in the run, the big fall salmon hold in the currents and make a move—or not—at the orange flies we struggle to cast over them. We know they are here because they have been in this place since time began. We see them jump now and then, and sometimes they rise to expose a fin or a tail and leave doughnut-shaped wakes that widen and diminish as they drift away.

These fish do not think like people, as they excite us with their near takes. But we have learned to think like them. And play like them. We will be here as long as the fish are showing.

It's another outdoor game, one on a side, fish and angler. In a sense these salmon hold us in a kind of servitude. In summer clothes, we cast and fight the subtle breezes and the evening dampness. Our small beach fire that crackles and snaps beneath a smoke-blackened tea pail makes dancing shadows against the yellowing swords of shore grass, the charcoal-treed hillside.

Before dark, my grandfather makes his way from the house down to the waterside. Papa likes to be among young people, to sit awhile by the fire, smoke a sailor's pipe, and tell us stories from his youth, still so fresh in his mind they could have happened only yesterday. Papa also wants to see if we have caught any fish that he can carry home and fillet for the salt barrel.

Papa is now a humble old man, feeble in appearance and homely dressed, though he was once a statuesque figure who had a proud temper and an air of authority, famed for his physical strength and endurance. (Although, according to my father, Papa was always a patient and submissive man around home.) He worked on the river drives and in the lumber woods until he was almost ninety years old, when his wonderful strength diminished and he was forced to resign himself to plaid house slippers and a parlour rocking chair.

Later in the evening, back in the farmhouse, by the light of a lamp and without glasses, he will read from his Bible—just as he does on Sunday evenings, from his candy-striped hammock erected between two trees, his big straw hat shading his eyes from the setting sun. He reads the Scripture because he has gotten religion in his old age, and also to exercise his mind. But here now, without shame he moves with the help of a walking stick. Above his flannel shirt collar and the top button of his fleece-lined underwear, there is a forest of grey hair; his trousers are held up with wide suspenders and no belt, his felt hat tilted over one ear. He pinches the noses of the children who come to sit on the bench and listen to him speak of the olden times. As he talks, he fills his pipe and lights it with one hand, one match.

Papa rests both arms upon his cane and starts a conversation with the words, "Well, now here's a funny thing, let me tell yuz," and he turns to spit, long reaching, into the tall grass. Then he tells us a tale of how, long ago, a Mi'kmaq maiden sat on the great rock at the mouth of the Renous River—Quarryville, then called Indiantown—and waited for her true love to come up the river by canoe. She had been promised his return after a land squabble was settled with the invading Europeans and, feeling that all was lost—her land, her way of life, her traditions—had pledged to wait for him, the only solid thing that remained in her life. While the Mi'kmaq were a kind and peaceful nation, the young maiden's lover was said to have been a high-spirited and daring warrior.

"Yes, she was a beautiful Indian girl and tanned as brown as the bark on that tree beside ya," Papa points to a spruce behind the bench.

She sat on the big rock, which was well out into the river and held on her bosom a bouquet of white flowers that looked like porcelain shirt buttons and were called Pearly Everlasting, said to have been an ornament of grace and purity. She fasted and prayed to the river gods to bring her lover back to her unharmed. She called his name into the night, hoping that his body and soul had the strength to endure.

But the gods were angry! And this was after a big fall rain, and the ill-tempered river, already swollen, was coming up fast, with the full-moon tides coming in from the gasping sea. Still, she would not move from the rock to escape the strengthening currents, as she had made a promise to her lover to meet him there, on this moon, on this night. The water came over her feet and on up past her waist and breasts, eventually sweeping her away, down the river in a sacrificial death.

She had become a martyr for her true love. And for her people's cause.

"It's the old Indian way, the old Indian spirit," Papa said.

This legend is all but forgotten here, except in the minds of the old. It's a tale to be rehashed at this time of year, on this river, its retelling inspired, no doubt, by the threat of rain. And the place name: Squaw Rock.

Papa said that, even to this day, on moonlit fall nights at the mouth of the Renous River, this young Aboriginal maiden can be glimpsed and sometimes heard, sitting out there on that big grey rock, waist-deep in water, crying to the river gods to bring her lover home.

And then, as if with a wish to escape the cooling autumn air, the old man heads back to the house by way of the cow pasture gate, limping as he goes, on worn shoes, his clothing grey like the charcoal shades of evening.

Because We Are Here

Here on the river, under a glass-like covering of crystal water, we can see the Atlantic salmon as they migrate upstream by the thousands, just as they have since the beginning of time. From our cabin windows we observe their habitual life patterns and mating rituals, and we feel the same old fascinations, if not greater, toward them with each passing year. It's as if each new sighting, each spectacular leaping fish we encounter, is the very last one we will see in our time; like old family who drop in to visit, like the homing robin or the resident crane, the salmon's return is always awe-inspiring to river people. And we set out to capture this magic as though it were a phenomenon of supernatural proportions.

It is because of the salmon that most of us live on the Miramichi. Regardless of our lineage, our station in life, our causes, we are aware of this fish's value here at home, its long journey abroad, the dangers encountered along the way, and its desire to make it back safely. And because we feel so close to this fish and its habitat, we cherish it, not as a game fish, not as a resource that will help us sell our real estate, not as a cause to raise money for large angling groups, not as something on the end of a line to be cranked in while it struggles for breath, but as a fellow river creature attempting to survive in this day of pollution, climate change, and the exploitation of our environment by so many international interests.

And yet, the fact that we—the river people—are still chasing after this fish, is a kind of paradox. Because we also have a tendency to use and sometimes even abuse the salmon, and this is in our bloodstreams and has been for generations; though, perhaps we do it not for the amusement in life so much, as for the sake of life itself. At times, we angle not for the sport of watching and feeling a fish get hooked and struggle on the end of our fishing line, rather we do it to catch a fish for the dinner table. And the fact that the salmon are still a part of our food supply, the conservation of this great fish is like a commitment which we are adamant about. Just like it was for our parents and grandparents—who were also born and raised here—the Atlantic salmon has been a part of our river people's livelihood for centuries. For we are makeshift river guides, portage men, outfitters, camp cooks, and sales people, and we have always needed the traditional big-dollar guests from away. Our lives have depended upon these fish and these people in one way or another since the river was settled by our forebears in the late seventeen and early eighteen hundreds. And because we are here, in good part, due to the abundance of the Atlantic salmon, the old lifestyle dies hard.

Through the centuries, we have learned to survive, without shame, off the river itself, and we are aware it is this great resource, this river business, that has helped to feed our families. So we encourage the foreign anglers to come to our river and try their luck, even while we keep a keen eye on our salmon stocks, a close watch on hook-and-release practices, good river ethics, and so on. While there are no high-brow environmentalists among us, no protesters, we are earth-friendly people. It is hard to be pretentious when we don't have deep pockets and we are faced with an uncertain future.

At the beginning of each new angling season, we follow the same routine that our parents and grandparents have set out. We repair our leaky boats and the coughing old outboard motors. We patch our tattered wading boots. We buy new clothing, along with our fishing, boat, and guiding licences, and we wait for the ice to break away and for the fish to come in from the sea. There is always a buzz along the river at this time of year. We talk about the clear-cuts in the forest, the snow melt, the runoff—which happens earlier each spring and with a greater inconsistency—the erosion and the ever-changing riverscape. Yes, we keep an eye on the river and on the well-being of the Atlantic salmon, for reasons of our own lives as much as for the fish. If there is a chance that this fish is in danger, a great sense of panic overtakes us. And there is much ado about the restocking process versus natural selection, the gene pool, the early run numbers, last year's catch, the "live release back into warm water" debate, the double-barbed hook and the use of landing nets as a way to lift a fish from the water, hold it up for a photograph.

There is also the rehashing of old fears about the incidental catch of high-sea trawlers, so far away, beyond our imaginations, beyond our control. And we wish our government would take up arms, if necessary, to protect our fish, our livelihood, and our heritage. Indeed, we harbour a zealous degree of protectionism when we feel our way of life is being threatened; it has been this way for as long as I can remember.

We are afraid of the international dollar, the deep-sea trawlers from foreign lands that could wipe out an entire fish run with one sweep of a drag net, and which just might threaten our river and our bay. Or the rivers and bays we leave to our children and grandchildren, all of whom, as we can see, are following in our footsteps.

Many of us are now old and looking for God. We are not able to angle in the big waters alone anymore. We don't like to venture that far afield unless it is in a dream. Or a memory. Our loose trousers are rolled up to reveal bird-like ankles, wobbly and unsure. Our one-time crops of thick hair have become scattered beneath the snows of a mountain top. And there is the exhaled stench of sweaty socks, the gravedigger's breath of homemade wines and tobacco smoke. Even with our sparrow hands firmly clamped to wading canes, we find that the underwater rocks, which are bald like so many dinosaur eggs and as slippery as cakes of wet toilet soap, are treacherous to step on, the currents too deep and too strong to chance our last days upon. We know that if we stumble and fall, we will be swept away, hopelessly, in a matter of seconds, while our unbelted chest waders fill up from the undertow, and we don't have the strength or the breath to kick them off. Yet, we want to keep our independence, our traditions, and we refuse to take a helping hand when we go to the river.

For the aged, the river flows a little faster, a little deeper, a little wider every day. Its crystal-clear waters course over that long and winding bed of polished stones through pools like the Mountain Channel, White Rapids, the Hell's Gates, and Bull's Run—from the mountainous logging town of Juniper in the centre of our province to the fishing village of Baie-Sainte-Anne, with its white clapboard lighthouses facing the sea, and where a thunder of waves breaks against the jagged cliffs between our beautiful white beaches that are fringed with yellow grasses. The river is a distance of some three hundred kilometres from end to end.

We maintain our occupations as trusty river guides who are willing to sit on the shore and coach some novice angler who has seen our paintings or read our books and is looking for a special day on the river, one that no one as yet has lived through or has tried to describe. They hope that their day on the water will be recorded for posterity. Because they want to be a part of the writings and paintings that have been glorified into a kind of fiction that emerges from the minds of long-term river inhabitants, the ones among us who have wandering imaginations. And the folklore of the old river itself, which is filled with magic. For there is always something positive in our art, something valuable in our age-old legacy, that has lured this person to our shores to be a part of the scene, to experience literally what has only been observed by virtue of the prose or the paintings of those of us who live here and who love the river as part of the home, or an intimate old friend. For every art lover, every reader is, while he is viewing or reading, the observer of his own self.

Still, it is always difficult to make a river event live up to the expectations we have laid out on canvas or described on the page. For through the years, these stories have been developed into a framed embroidery, an art form of hereditary reflection, remembered and forgotten and remembered again for the hundredth time and which has become enhanced by the inner theatre of the local mindset. For the genius of the artisan is always exaggerated at least a little, and reality, the current-day expedition, however rewarding, never measures up to what we have captured in our art. It's impossible to analogize—even to those with the most nurtured imaginations—on the river or in the mind.

River Art

Now our destiny has become more obvious, more dramatic, and yes, more final, because we, the river people, are more mature, more sensitive, and indeed more reconciled. We have grown aware of the value of our time and place, as the few years we have left slip through our aged and bloodless hands. For us, life has become slower, less eventful, while time itself has quickened. And the accolades we have sought for so many years are slipping by us, one by one. It's like watching the scenery from the window of a moving train and reaching out to grasp a favourite wildflower or a blueberry in passing, hoping that our senses are still keen enough to appreciate its childhood fragrance or taste. Only to find that its sweetness was not in the flower or the berry, rather in our minds.

This could be described as the unsettled season at the end of summer.

While parts of our bodies have become languid and mute, and we have grown hard of hearing, hard of smelling, and hard of sight, we have matured internally, and many of us have taken to some new form of meditation and/or prayer. We now look at life, the bit that remains, not as something to be celebrated in a frivolous and foolish manner, and certainly not in the destruction of earthly or river things—the brutish indifference we practised years ago to satisfy our youthful desires—but as a time and place to be studied and recorded in our paintings and our journals. So that all we have learned through the years may be taken as a lesson to those who follow us along this windy voyage. Having survived a few shipwrecks along the way, we hope that our message is appreciated and that no one will consciously repeat our mistakes.

River Art, I call it.

We observe as the events of each new day repeat themselves. As do those of the seasons of the year, the seasons of life. We now stand and listen intently for the subtle whisper of the pine trees when a river breeze touches them on a spring day. It's like old times, when we could hear a little tune the wind made as it pushed through the screen doors in our farmhouse kitchens. And we strain, with a hand behind an ear, to celebrate once more the singing of an April song sparrow, "comeandeat, comeandeat, comeandeat." That familiar air brings with it an adolescent time and place; the solitary fears of puberty, the drama of first love, so long ago they return now not in dreams but in the memories of dreams.

We inhale the centuries-old drowsiness of our river's former communities at two in the afternoon, under the sun's burning winds, so penetrating they turn our skin into dried-up plums, and because we are care-worn and weak from our long years of mental and physical toil, we finally confront our fears and weaknesses. Where do we go from here? How much longer can we go on? What will be left of us in a few short years? What quality will our lives have as we grow nearer to death? For we are not afraid of dying, rather of living too long in poor conditions, poor health. And we clear a place on some wooded hillside—perhaps overlooking Morse Brook—for the resting place of our ashes.

Even at this age, especially at this age, we learn things we didn't know about ourselves, the admiration we had for who we thought we were in youth, our acclaimed virtues, our true weaknesses that have grown with us and are now so obvious. Except for our names, through the years we have changed completely into different people, souls who are living in dissimilar places, yet carrying the same old personal identity: our birth certificates, driver's licences, and Social Insurance Numbers. Though perhaps we are humbled by the thoughts of our misguided youth and former arrogance. And we have grown to appreciate different social habits, different priorities as the aging mind reaches for the subtleties that were once unappreciated, if they were ever visible at all.

Looking back on our former selves is like going to that old place to meet a friend we knew in the past, or thought we knew, only to find him shallow and uncaring, without a cause or an intended legacy, and we wonder why anyone would have befriended that person at all, or why, indeed, he had tried to bond with a person of our kind. We are in no way alike, and we have been walking on different paths for over a half-century.

I battle my long-suffered allergies as I unconsciously breathe in the sweet-scented fields of mown hay, the listless river haze, the shore meadow's delicate hues that are, oh so quickly, being thrown into contrast by fields that ripen for the harvest. And I shiver at the first sight of the early morning frost that turns the little nettles of interval grass into wigs of steel wool, and then to cotton from a dusting of snow, because I realize that these are the official proofs, the thumbprints of autumn, and an eternal winter is not far off.

I stare with a sense of melancholy as the red, yellow, and brown maple leaves are windswept from our former dooryards to lodge along the line fences of December farms before the coming of the snow. This is a breeze that whistles right through our clothing, our bodies, and our souls. And because I feel that I am now something less than whole—that all of us here are less than the men and women we once were, physically at least—I struggle against an urge to retreat into hermitage; we all want to be remembered as being wholesome and carefree. While the years have done a number on us, it does not alter the way our acquaintances remember us from our youth. We are now less brilliant than we were in old photographs or their time-enhanced memories. Our clothes are too big on our bony frames, our eyes are glassy and moist, and our backs are stooped beneath bat-wing umbrellas, destroying the perceptions from long ago, so that at reunions, which we go to with reluctance, we have to wear name tags to reveal the person we once were.

I have also become more aware of, sometimes even frightened by, those internal, arthritic rains, the autumnal gales of amnesia, the dark swirling clouds of insomnia, and the stiff and pessimistic graveyard winds of the approaching season that fills my soul with so much uncertainty; each year a bit more dramatic than the last. For nothing reveals a person's character more clearly than the humbleness in which he faces death. And as I walk at nightfall, I pause to observe the blue, moonlit skies of early winter, the stars that twinkle in their places, the thin shadows of power lines cast upon new snow after the plow has passed—telephone cables which are laden with fluffy white coats to make them look like uncarded strands of wool or tubes mittened in rabbit furs that stretch between roadside crosses, to be shaken free by a gentle breeze or the perch of a night owl, that bird of wisdom and destiny. I watch these things with a sense of foreboding. And, condemned to oblivion, I struggle with a new-found awareness of the demographic I am now a part of, while in my old-horse wisdom I try to fathom where I go from here.

And suddenly I am overcome with the realization that there is no physical place to go, and so I turn to the past for a bit of old-time comfort and warmth, because my memories now matter more to me than my short-lived visions of the future, my memories and the grace of the Holy Spirit.

In sequence, I rehash my former good experiences as though they are the replaying of old country movies (complete with our Dylan music, McKuen poetry, and bohemian clothes and hairstyles), watch through the shadows of my cataracts while it's all being recycled, in black and white, for the hundredth time, while expecting the sad if not the happy ending to have changed since I last saw it. Or perhaps hoping that I have changed or have forgotten how it ends—for a movie is old only if you can remember seeing it before. Once there, I stay in these comfortable places for hours, even days. Maybe I have learned how better to handle the outcome, or perhaps I have subconsciously embellished it. Like writing fiction, this is a kind of guided learning, always positive and somewhere in back of me. The way that memory (and a bit of substance abuse) embroider the past, making from this distance perfection out of mediocrity. Just some little change here and there is all I ask for, something I can undo in my mind to prevent me from inheriting the legacy of being an idle fool.

I don't exactly trust nostalgia to correct these wrongs.

But each time I go back to one of those early experiences, I hear the same foolish laughs, the same dreadful moans from the thorny wounds of a past that cannot be changed however I look at it. I cringe at the mean-spirited person I was back then: careless, greedy, arrogant, an egoist, and an abuser of the environment. And I wonder, was that really me? I think of the wildlife I unnecessarily killed to enhance my caveman reputation as a successful provider or a famous outdoor person. And I break into a sweat because I can now see that it was done for the primitive pleasure that came with outsmarting a beast, having that fish, that bird, or that wild animal fall to my prey. Yes, I found glory in this and in my mind felt that my talents, though basic—and certainly uncultivated—should have been put on display. I justified this by telling myself that the meat was needed if my family were to survive here on the river, and someone had to look after, even entertain the rest— though far too loud and too often—to make life a bit more endearing. And yes, I wanted to be seen. It is not easy to come to terms with one's own ghost.

In spite of all this, sadly those were probably my happiest years, lived to the fullest without conscience, or guilt, either human or divine.

I finally realize that it is better not to dwell on the past for too long, that one should not be too hard on one's self because the times have changed and that part of me is from another day, another country, another people. I could not have lived my life according to the future. Neither can I reverse the past, that old way of thinking, to suit the modern ways in which I am living today. I pray that historians will be kind to me.

In my declining years, I also have developed contempt for danger, which becomes more obvious as time goes by; for each day lived, I have less to lose. My past life, though flawed, is now being enhanced by the magic of embroidery and is more valuable than any future I will encounter from here on, literally or metaphorically. So I nurture a new-found selflessness and a life-giving generosity to tell of my life's meditations in my own words before they are lost.

Hardened by the ingratitudes of life, I now have no use for materialistic people. (Of course, I was never a social climber, nor do I look for fame, rather some small form of acceptance if not recognition.) I no longer measure my own successes—some never have—in terms of money earned or things acquired; rather, I want to make a difference, create a positive mark, leave a few tracks. And I hope that these hard-learned lessons, these causes, are remembered by those who matter most when I am gone.

Say what you will, there is good value in my experienced example. And I feel a need to protect my true heritage, my legacy, my culture, however humble. Because I have discovered along the way that true riches are not to be measured in "things." I have long since turned to the arts of life—peasant art, folk art, river art, call it what you like.

However, we do not celebrate life for art's sake, rather art for life's sake.

In our now-abandoned farmhouses, river places that were once filled with our large families and where the spiritual life of the assemblage revolved in former times, the invisible, upright pianos stand in front parlours. And if we listen carefully, we can hear the silent music of a Christmas Eve, the schoolhouse recitations performed by a hearth fire, the cheerful, yet melancholy laughter of so many families under one roof. There is a sense of warmth enkindled from the ashes of a mantel destroyed a half-century ago. As we crunch on glass and falling plaster, are spooked by a blowing gauze curtain, we can still taste the home cooking, smell the unemptied chamber pots, see the clouds of cobwebs that smother our one-time perspectives, old hangings which now cling to the walls of exposed lattice.

The dam, the covered bridge, the boat, the pine tree, the

ice jam, and a dozen more attempts in trying to capture the splendour of the river and the leaping salmon. Some of us may step dance, draw, paint, weave, play an instrument, sing, or write; it's all an expression of the river's culture and art to be captured in its own distinct way and passed along from hand to hand and relived down the road.

These pieces of art, some of which are yet to be conceived, are like reoccurring dreams, old loves that flash through our minds, one, three, two in the order of their personal greatness. They are loves, not romances. We must not admit to romantic errors. No, we are too practical, too deep-rooted for that. We grasp the heartstrings as we feel them and attempt to display them on paper, canvas, or in a handwoven tapestry.

And these works of art were not meant to make reality vanish into shades of romanticism, rather to carry the truth forward while rejecting all that was not heartfelt. For art is a lasting impression, and life itself, as we know, is short-lived.

In some ways, it's as though we are chiselling the epitaph on our own gravestone.

But suddenly we find comfort in the hope that while we, the river artists, may die, what surely will live on is the artistic causes to which we have dedicated our lives, the warmth of our oldest and greatest memories, without glory, but purified by time and solitude.

We now show more respect toward our fellow river creatures, and we refuse to stand and watch anyone abuse or degrade them. In a sense we have become people of virtue, people of sensitivity, cerebral, nature-loving souls. Finally. And this has helped us to appreciate the finer things in life, which of course are our true heart feelings. Because we believe that God and the heart are where real life and true art are conceived. And not to be trivialized or commercialized, because we do it for the love of life, the love of each other, the love of truth and our river.

Like all true artisans, we have sought out our deepest feelings and have tried our best to follow them. They are like recollections of our past loves. Because in our minds this mission, this need to record our history, is an inspiration that, at this age, is spawned from nothing short of Divine Providence.

Acknowledgements

The essay titled "Spring Waters Run Deep" has appeared in part under the name "Miramichi Spring" in the *Atlantic Salmon Journal*, Summer 2009, and "The Old Fishing Hole" in the *Nashwaak Review*, Summer/Fall 2009. Also published in the *Atlantic Salmon Journal* were the essays: "On The Cains," which appeared under the name "Time Travel—A River Of Memories Flows By With Each Stroke Of The Paddle," 2008; "At Papa's Rock," 2009; "Autumnal River" appeared as "Autumn River," with photos by Tom Montgomery, 2009. The latter was a finalist in the Writers' Federation of New Brunswick's 2011 Literary Competition and was nominated for an Atlantic Journalism Award in 2010. The essay "Why We Are Here" was published in the *Atlantic Salmon Journal* under the name "Past Perfect" in 2009. "River Art" was published in the *Atlantic Salmon Journal* under the title "River Canvas," with art work by Audrey Purcell, in 2010.

I would like to thank the New Brunswick Arts Board for fellowships received during the writing of this book.

I would also like to thank David Adams Richards, Tony Tremblay, Dennis Duffy, John Timmins, Martin Silverstone, Kal Kotkas, and Larry Kennedy for their technical assistance while I was writing this memoir. And thank you to editors James Duplacey, Rebecca Leaman, and Paula Sarson.

I would like to acknowledge the sources of the following material. Every effort has been made to secure permission for excerpts reproduced in this book:

p. 63 Excerpt from "Gooseberries" by Anton Chekhov, from *Selected Stories of Anton Chehkov*, trans. Richard Pevear and Larissa Volokhonsky. (Random House, 2000).

p. 74 Song lyrics from traditional song "The North Atlantic Squadron."

p. 83 Excerpt from "Birches" by Robert Frost, from *Mountain Interval.* Reprinted by permission of Henry Holt & Company.

p. 84 Song lyrics from traditional song "Darling Nelly Gray" by B.R. Hanby.

p. 88 Excerpt from "A Boring Story from an Old Man's Notes" by Anton Chekhov, from *Selected Stories of Anton Chekhov*, trans. Richard Pevear and Larissa Volokhonsky. (Random House, 2000).

p. 97 Song lyrics from "Now Is the Hour" by Clement Scott, Maewa Kaihau, and Dorothy Stewart.

p. 156 Excerpt from *Angle of Repose* by Wallace Stegner (London: Penguin, 2000).

p. 172 & 199 Excerpts from *Heart of Darkness* by Joseph Conrad (New York: Modern Library, 1999).

p. 175 Excerpt from "My Heart Leaps Up" by William Wordsworth, from *William Wordsworth: Selected Poetry and Prose*, edited by Geoffrey H. Hartman (New York: New American Library, 1970).

p. 183 Song lyrics from traditional song "Rolling Home to Dear Old England."

p. 203 Excerpt from *The Kreutzer Sonata* by Leo Tolstoy, trans. David McDuff. Reprinted by permission of Penguin.

p. 204 Excerpt from "The Death of the Hired Man" by Robert Frost, from *North of Boston.* Reprinted by permission of Henry Holt & Company.

p. 205 Excerpt from *Wolf Willow: A History, A Story, and A Memory of the Last Plains Frontier* by Wallace Stegner (London: Penguin, 1990).

p. 206 Excerpt from "Ode: Intimations of Immortality" by William Wordsworth from *Recollections of Early Childhood William Wordsworth Selected Poetry and Prose,* edited by Geoffrey H. Hartman (New York: New American Library, 1970).

Photo: Harvey Studios

Books in Canada described Wayne Curtis' work as "a pleasure to read, for no detail escapes his discerning eye." The author of many novels, story collections, and non-fiction works, he has also won the David Adams Richards Award for short fiction as well as the Woodcock Award and the CBC Drama Award. Curtis has been a contributor to *The National Post* and *The Globe and Mail* as well as magazines such as *Quill and & Quire* and *Outdoor Canada.* His stories have appeared in *The Fiddlehead, The Cormorant,* and *The Antigonish Review,* among other publications, and been dramatized on CBC Radio and CBC Television. Wayne currently divides his time between the Miramichi River and Fredericton, New Brunswick.